C000152982

C I T Y P A C K
Atlanta

By Mark Beffart

Fodor's

Fodor's Travel Publications, Inc.
New York • Toronto • London • Sydney • Auckland

© 1996 by The Automobile Association
Maps copyright 1996 © by The Automobile Association
Fold-out map:
    © RV Reise- und Verkehrsverlag Munich . Stuttgart
    © Cartography: GeoData

Page 1: Downtown Atlanta

Page 2 (above): the Carter Presidential Center

Page 5 (a): Center for Puppetry Arts
Page 5 (b): on the steps of Ebenezer Church

Page 13 (a): Six Flags Over Georgia
Page 13 (b): Hall of Flags, State Capitol of Georgia

Page 23: Atlanta History Center

Page 49 (a): The World of Coca-Cola
Page 49 (b) Flatiron Building

Page 61 (a): High Museum of Folk Art
Page 61 (b): Buckhead

Page 87 (a): rush hour traffic on the Interstate
Page 87 (b): Intersection

Published in the United States by Fodor's Travel Publications, Inc.
Published in the United Kingdom by AA Publishing

Fodor's is a trademark of Fodor's Travel Publications, Inc.

ISBN 0-679-02956-7
First Edition

Fodor's Citypack Atlanta

Author: Mark Beffart
Cartography: The Automobile Association
      RV Reise- und Verkehrsverlag
Cover Design: Tigist Getachew, Fabrizio La Rocca
Cover Photograph (raft): Georgia Department of Industry, Trade & Tourism

Special Sales
Fodor's Travel Publications are available at special discounts for bulk purchases (100 copies or more) for sales promotions or premiums. Special editions, including personalized covers, excerpts of existing guides, and corporate imprints, can be created in large quantities for special needs. For more information write to Special Marketing, Fodor's Travel Publications, 201 East 50th St., New York NY 10022.

Color separation by BTB Colour Reproduction Ltd, Whitchurch, Hampshire.
Manufactured by Dai Nippon Printing Co. (Hong Kong) Ltd

10 9 8 7 6 5 4 3

Contents

About this book

Citypack Atlanta is divided into six sections to cover the six most important aspects of your visit to Atlanta.

1. ATLANTA LIFE *(pages 5–12)*
Your personal introduction to Atlanta by author Mark Beffart
Facts and figures
Leading characters
The big events in Atlanta's history

2. HOW TO ORGANIZE YOUR TIME *(pages 13–22)*
Make the most of your time in Atlanta
4 one-day itineraries
2 suggested walks
2 evening strolls
4 excursions beyond the city
Calendar of events

3. ATLANTA'S TOP 25 SIGHTS *(pages 23–48)*
Your concise guide to sightseeing
Mark Beffart's own choice, including his personal introduction to each sight
Description and history
Highlights of each attraction
Comprehensive practical information
Each sight located on the inside cover of the book

4. ATLANTA'S BEST *(pages 49–60)*
What Atlanta is renowned for
Modern Architecture, Oldest Buildings, Museums, Battle of Atlanta Sites, Attractions for Children, Free Attractions, Neighborhoods, Parks & Forests African-American Attractions
Practical details throughout

5. ATLANTA: WHERE TO... *(pages 61–86)*
The best places to eat, shop, be entertained, and stay
8 categories of restaurant
8 categories of store
6 categories of entertainment venue
3 categories of hotel
Price bands and booking details

6. ATLANTA TRAVEL FACTS *(pages 87–94)*
Essential information for your stay

SYMBOLS

Throughout the guide a few straightforward symbols are used to denote the following categories

🚼 map reference on the fold-out map accompanying this book (see below)

✉ address

☎ telephone number

🕐 opening times

🍴 restaurant or café on premises or nearby

🚇 nearest subway station

🚌 nearest bus/trolleybus/trolley route

🚊 nearest overground train station

♿ facilities for visitors with disabilities

🎫 admission charge

↔ other places of interest nearby

❓ tours, lectures, or special events

➤ indicates the page where you will find a fuller description

MAPS

All map references are to the separate fold-out map accompanying this book. For example, the State Capitol of Georgia in Washington Street has the following information 🚼 F7—indicating the grid square in which the State Capitol of Georgia will be found. All entries within the Top 25 Sights section are also plotted by number (not page number) on the downtown plan located on the inside front and back covers of this book.

PRICES

Where appropriate, the cost of an establishment is indicated by $ signs: $$$ denotes higher prices; $$ denotes average prices; $ denotes lower charges.

ATLANTA
life

A PERSONAL VIEW

Beckoning city

I never get tired of Atlanta's modern skyline. To see it first when you enter the city, especially from the south or north, is a magnificent sight. As you reach the crest of a hill, it appears like a beacon, towers of varying sizes and shapes gleaming in the sunlight, jabbing at the sky, a dramatic symbol of Atlanta's success.

In 1959, in the heat of the Civil Rights debates, Mayor William B. Hartsfield proudly called Atlanta "the city too busy to hate." Two years later, while blacks were still being arrested in demonstrations across the South, Atlanta became the first southern city peacefully to desegregate its schools.

This slogan marks the essence of Atlanta's history. It has always been a busy city, not willing to remain in the past, but moving forward at a rapid rate, shrewd entrepreneurs adding to the success of other entrepreneurs. After 90 percent of Atlanta was destroyed (1864) in the Civil War, it was quickly rebuilt, becoming a "brave and beautiful city" as noted in 1886 by *Atlanta Constitution* editor Henry Grady.

Today, its nicknames of Hotlanta, The Big A, Capital of the New South, and the International Gateway City, along with its distinctive modern skyline, evoke visions of a dynamic and progressive city. As you fly over Atlanta, a vast city spreads out in all directions, evidence of a phenomenal growth rate that has seen the population double since 1975. Then called the five county metropolitan area by the Chamber of Commerce, it today boasts over 3 million people living in over 20 counties encompassing 6,150 square miles and 111 suburban towns—and is still expanding.

Come to Atlanta expecting to be greatly surprised. The Old South, as dramatized by the novel and movie *Gone with the Wind*, doesn't exist here. Due to several public relations campaigns, Atlanta has attracted people from every state and numerous foreign countries.

Downtown Atlanta

Inside the Fox Theatre

International immigration

The signs of Atlanta's progress are seen everywhere. As an international city, its best example is in the suburb of Chamblee, located a short distance southwest of the I-85/I-285 intersection. Fifteen years ago, this community had a primarily white-only, working-class population. Today, it has one of the largest Asian communities in the United States.

This fusion of ardent southerners with its new neighbors gives the city a unique character, a combination of southern charm mixed with a dose of northern brashness and worldly sophistication. Atlanta is not a typical southern city, slow and backward as portrayed by Hollywood. The pace here is fast, easily attested from the moment you enter its multilane interstate highway system that crisscrosses and circles the city.

Despite its pace, Atlanta is a fun and hospitable place to visit. From walking tours in its beautiful neighborhoods, to visiting historical sights and high-tech attractions, to restaurants serving every possible cuisine, to a vibrant entertainment scene with Broadway theater, music concerts, ballet, and professional sports, there is no room for boredom here. Atlanta is a city with something for everyone.

ATLANTA IN FIGURES

GENERAL INFORMATION

- Atlanta is 1,050 feet above sea level, the highest elevation of any major U.S. city east of the Mississippi River.
- The highest point in Atlanta is on Peachtree Street between Ellis Street and International Boulevard.
- Atlanta is located 33°45'10" latitude north, a similar latitude to North Africa.
- Atlanta is the 12th largest metropolitan area in the United States with over 3 million people, yet only 394,017 people (1990 census) live within the Atlanta city limits, making it only the 36th largest city.
- The Atlanta metropolitan area consists of 6,150 square miles, 20 counties, and 111 suburban towns.
- Sixty-four percent of Atlantans own their own home and land.
- The average Atlanta resident takes 56 minutes to commute from home to place of employment.
- African-Americans comprise approximately 65 percent of the Atlanta city population.
- Over 95,000 students attend Atlanta's 42 colleges, universities, technical institutes, and seminaries.

ATLANTA COMMERCE

- Underground Atlanta is Atlanta's most popular tourist attraction with over 13 million annual visitors.
- Seven hundred thirty of the *Fortune* 1,000 companies have offices in Atlanta.
- More than 1,200 foreign businesses operate in Atlanta and 48 countries have representation through consulates and trade offices.
- Sales tax on most retail goods and services is 6 percent in Atlanta, 4–5 percent in the suburbs.
- None of the famous movie *Gone with the Wind* was filmed in Georgia.
- Lenox Square Mall is the largest enclosed shopping mall in the South with over 14 million annual visitors.
- Fifty percent of Georgia's physicians practice medicine in the metropolitan Atlanta area.

ATLANTA PEOPLE

HANK AARON (b. 1934)

Baseball star Hank Aaron is Atlanta's most famous professional athlete. On April 8, 1974, this Atlanta Braves outfielder claimed his place in sports history by hitting home run number 715, which broke Babe Ruth's record that had stood for 37 years. "The Hammer", or "Hammering Hank," as he was known during his career, went on to hit another 40 home runs before he retired from active playing in 1976. He is also the all-time leader for runs batted in (2,297), second in runs scored (2,174), and third in hits (3,771). In 1982, his first year of eligibility, he was elected to the Baseball Hall of Fame. Today, he is a vice president of the Braves.

JIMMY CARTER (b. 1924)

After a brief term as a state legislator in the 1960s, Jimmy Carter, a peanut farmer from the south central Georgia town of Plains, became in 1971 the 76th governor of Georgia. Five years later in November 1976, he was elected as the 39th President of the United States. Although he was unable to solve all of the country's problems during his administration (1977–1981), his work afterwards with Habitat for Humanity and the Carter Presidential Center (▶ 35) has thrust him into the spotlight. Today he is in demand as a peace negotiator (in recent years concerning the conflicts in Korea, Bosnia, Haiti, and various African nations) and a conference speaker.

CORETTA SCOTT KING (b. 1928)

The widow of Martin Luther King, Jr. has done more than anyone to further the legacy and philosophy of the slain Civil Rights leader. Shortly after his 1968 assassination in Memphis, Tennessee, she established the Martin Luther King, Jr. Center for Non-Violent Social Change, which is visited by thousands of people every year to view King's tomb and to attend conferences on various Civil Rights and black culture topics. She is active in many Civil Rights organizations and has traveled the world to promote her husband's ideas.

Ted Turner

Ted Turner (b.1938)

Atlanta's richest man is known as a "maverick" and a "gambler." Taking incredible risks and ignoring his critics, he exploited an inheritance from his father's billboard company in the late 1960s, turning a small independent television station into what is now billed as the "Superstation." In the mid-1970s, using station profits, he bought a major-league baseball team (Braves) and a basketball team (Hawks). In the 1980s, after failing to buy one of the primary television networks, he carved out his own media empire by creating the 24-hour news network CNN, followed by Headline News and several other cable networks. He also owns 6,700 MGM movies.

A CHRONOLOGY

1782 | British explorers discover the Creek village of Standing Indian at the confluence of the Chattahoochee River and Peachtree Creek.

1812 | Fort Gilmer, a Federal militia outpost, is established at Standing Indian to protect settlers from the Creeks.

1826 | Surveyors suggest the Atlanta area for a railroad to connect the state with northern markets.

1833 | Hardy Ivy, Atlanta's first permanent settler, builds a log cabin on the present-day site of Courtland and Ellis Streets (Downtown).

1837 | Stephen H. Long, a military engineer, marks the terminus of the state-owned Western Atlantic Railroad with the "Zero Milepost," and a tiny village named Terminus begins to grow.

1843 | Terminus is renamed Marthasville after popular ex-governor Wilson Lumpkin's daughter Martha.

1845 | Marthasville is renamed Atlanta.

1847 | Atlanta is officially incorporated as a city.

1860 | Atlanta's population reaches 10,000.

1861 | Georgia secedes from the Union and joins the Confederacy.

1864 | Union armies under General William Tecumseh Sherman lay siege to Atlanta for two months, destroying 90 percent of the city .

1868 | Atlanta becomes the capital of Georgia.

1870 | Georgia is readmitted into the United States Union, the last seceded Confederate state to gain reentry.

1886 | Pharmacist John S. Pemberton creates a new headache remedy called Coca-Cola.

1900 | Professor E. B. DuBois founds the National

Association for the Advancement of Colored People (NAACP). Population is now 90,000.

1917 A fire destroys 1,938 buildings, making 10,000 people homeless and claiming one fatality.

1920 Atlanta's population grows to 200,000 people.

1929 Atlanta opens its first airport, Candler Field, on the site of a former car race track.

1936 Margaret Mitchell's novel *Gone with the Wind* is published. Over one million copies are sold by the year's end.

1939 The movie version of *Gone with the Wind* premières in Atlanta at the Loews Grand Theater. Black cast members and other blacks are not allowed to attend due to segregation laws.

1959 Sit-ins, boycotts, and riots protesting the segregation of blacks from white schools and other establishments begin in Atlanta.

1964 Martin Luther King, Jr. wins the Nobel Prize for Peace. The Beatles perform at Atlanta Stadium.

1966 The Braves major-league baseball franchise moves to Atlanta from Milwaukee. The Falcons National Football League team begins its first year in Atlanta.

1968 The funeral of assassinated Martin Luther King, Jr. is held in Atlanta.

1971 Jimmy Carter is elected Governor of Georgia.

1974 Maynard Jackson is elected Atlanta's first black mayor.

1979 MARTA Rapid Rail (subway–elevated train system) opens for business.

1983 Martin Luther King, Jr.'s birthday becomes a national holiday.

1988 Atlanta hosts the Democratic National Convention.

1996 Atlanta hosts the 26th Summer Olympics.

People & Events from History

The Battle of Atlanta, 1864

SIEGE OF ATLANTA IN 1864

The Union army laid siege to Atlanta from July 22 to August 22. The heaviest bombardment occurred in the period August 9–11 as eleven Union batteries and ten Confederate units fought against each other. During this period, the city was an inferno as over 5,000 shells struck it, reducing it to rubble. One onlooker wrote that "...all the fires of hell, and all the thunders of the universe seemed to be blazing and roaring over Atlanta." Amazingly, only 20 citizens were killed during the shelling.

THE COCA-COLA COMPANY

The most renowned beverage in the world was originally developed as a headache remedy in 1886 by pharmacist John S. Pemberton. Frank Robinson, one of Pemberton's partners, crafted the famous script still used in its trademark and named the drink after its two primary ingredients, the coca leaf and kola nut. Pemberton could not foresee its potential and subsequently sold the formula to Asa Candler in 1891 for $2,300. A merchandising wizard, Candler developed Coca-Cola into Atlanta's most prosperous company, selling it for $25 million in 1919 to a group headed by Ernest Woodruff.

ASSASSINATION OF MARTIN LUTHER KING, JR.

When Martin Luther King, Jr. was assassinated in 1968, black neighborhoods broke into riots across the nation. As Atlanta prepared for the funeral, they also prepared for violence, an act King preached against. Mayor Ivan Allen was instructed by Robert Woodruff, the President of Coca-Cola, to do whatever was right and necessary to honor the slain leader, promising to absorb whatever costs the city could not handle. Over 200,000 persons, black and white, rich and poor, celebrities and the unknown, marched in the funeral procession.

Andrew Young (b.1932)

Since the assassination of Martin Luther King, Jr. in 1968, a number of black leaders have picked up the torch of the Civil Rights movement. In Atlanta, Andrew Young is the most prominent. In 1972, he became the first black in the U.S. Congress since the late 1860s, serving until 1977 when he was named Ambassador to the United Nations. In 1981, he became Mayor of Atlanta, a post he held until 1989. As a consummate promoter, he has done more than any other person in the past 20 years to bring worldwide attention to Atlanta.

ATLANTA
how to organize your time

13

ITINERARIES

Atlanta is a sprawling city that is best divided into smaller sections for touring. For easy division, spend a day each visiting the sights near its three main business districts: Downtown, Midtown, and Buckhead, all accessible by public transportation. Then explore some of its interesting neighborhoods and suburban sights.

ITINERARY ONE	DOWNTOWN
	Downtown Atlanta contains some of the city's most interesting sights and attractions.
Breakfast	Start with an early breakfast at your hotel.
Morning	Visit the State Capitol of Georgia (➤ 27). Walk down Martin Luther King, Jr. Drive to The World of Coca-Cola (➤ 28).Cross Depot Plaza to Underground Atlanta (➤ 29).
Lunch	Mick's (➤ 63) on the Upper Alabama Street level.
Afternoon	Visit Atlanta Heritage Row (➤ 30) and the Olympic Experience (➤ 29). From Five Points station, take MARTA train to the CNN Center (➤ 31).
ITINERARY TWO	MIDTOWN
	Midtown is the cultural center of Atlanta with the city's art museum and famed Fox Theatre.
Breakfast	Doughnuts and coffee at Krispy Kreme (295 Ponce de Leon Avenue).
Morning	Exit left, and walk a half mile or take bus 2 to Peachtree Street. Turn right to Road to Tara Museum (➤ 42) and Fox Theatre (➤ 41) across street. Behind Fox Theatre enter modern building to Telephone Museum (➤ 54).
Lunch	The Varsity (➤ 63), Atlanta's most famous cheap eatery, is only three blocks from here.
Afternoon	Take train from North Avenue station to Arts Center (N5) for High Museum of Art (➤ 43). Walk through Ansley Park neighborhood (➤ 58) for one mile or take a taxi to Atlanta Botanical Garden (➤ 44).

ITINERARIES

ITINERARY THREE	BUCKHEAD

Buckhead is a favorite area of Atlantans to shop, dine, and party.

Breakfast

Coffee and pastries at Café Intermezzo Coffeehouse (145 Peachtree Road).

Morning

Explore the art galleries, antiques, and decorative furnishings stores on Bennett Street (➤ 72). Take bus 23 to Pharr Road. Walk down Pharr Road to Oxford Books (➤ 74). Turn left on Buckhead Avenue, behind the store, to reach Fay Gold Gallery (➤ 73). Cross to Bolling Way lined with clubs to East Paces Ferry Road lined with more clubs, stores, and galleries.

Lunch

Take bus 40 to Atlanta History Center (➤ 46) and dine at their Coach House Restaurant (11:30–2:30).

Afternoon

Tour Atlanta History Center sights. Take bus 40 or 58 to Georgia Governor's Mansion (➤ 47). Return to Peachtree Street and take bus 23 to Lenox Square Mall.

ITINERARY FOUR ATLANTA NEIGHBORHOODS

Atlanta sights are spread all over the city, some dispersed within its beautiful neighborhoods.

Breakfast

M.O.C.H.A. coffee-house (1424 North Highland Avenue, near University Drive).

Morning

Follow North Highland Avenue or take bus 16 through the chic Virginia-Highland neighborhood (➤ 58) to the Carter Presidential Center, about two miles (➤ 35). Little Five Points (➤ 18) is a ten-minute walk from the Center. Walk down Euclid Avenue to Inman Park (➤ 34).

Lunch

Burton's Grill (➤ 62).

Afternoon

Take MARTA to the Candler Park station and bus 6 to Michael C. Carlos Museum (➤ 48). Follow Clifton Road to the Fernbank Museum of Natural History (➤ 36).

15

WALKS

THE SIGHTS

INFORMATION

Distance 4 miles
Time 40–60 minutes (no stops); 2–4 hours to take time to view inside buildings and sights
Start point Underground Atlanta
✚ F7
✉ Peachtree Street at Upper Alabama Street
🚇 Five Points (0)
End point Midtown
✚ F5
✉ Peachtree Street at North Avenue
🚇 North Avenue (N3)

16

PEACHTREE STREET: DOWNTOWN

Since Atlanta's original charter, Peachtree Street has been the spine and major thoroughfare of the city. Beginning at Underground Atlanta, follow it north to Five Points, the heart of Atlanta's financial district, named after the convergence of Peachtree Street (twice, N and S), Decatur Street (E), Marietta Street (W), and Edgewood Avenue (NE). At the Marietta corner is the 43-storey Wachovia Bank of Georgia Tower situated on the site of Jacob's Drug Store where Coca-Cola was first served as a fountain drink in 1886. Georgia State University, a few blocks to the right, contains the Mercer Music Collection. A half block north on Peachtree Street is the newly landscaped Woodruff Park, with the 52-story, rusty-colored Georgia-Pacific Building in the background. A right turn on to Auburn Avenue, at the top of the park, leads to the Martin Luther King, Jr. National Historic District.

Business, shopping, and culture Continuing north on Peachtree Street, take a look at the triangular Flatiron Building and elaborately decorated Candler Building. Opposite the latter is the High Museum of Art Folk Art and Photography Galleries in the Georgia-Pacific Building. To the left across Peachtree Street is the tiny Margaret Mitchell Park and the cubist-looking Atlanta-Fulton County Public Library. Ahead is the shiny 73-story cylindrical Westin Peachtree Plaza Hotel and the One Ninety One Peachtree Tower with its funky neoclassical top. At opposite Ellis Street corners, peep into the luxurious Ritz-Carlton Hotel and Macy's department store. For an early lunch, stop at the Hard Rock Cafe (Peachtree Street at International Boulevard) or one of many restaurants a half block farther north at The Mall at the Peachtree Center. One block left (west) via International Boulevard is the new Welcome South Center, with tourist bureau for eight southern states, a travel bookstore and a Thomas Cook foreign exchange.

WALKS

PEACHTREE STREET: MIDTOWN

Continue to walk north along Peachtree Street
past the Hyatt Regency Atlanta Hotel to Ralph
McGill Boulevard, where a right turn will take
you to SciTrek, or you may wish to continue
on to the Atlanta Museum. Ahead to the left
is the NationsBank Plaza Tower, the tallest
building in the South. If you haven't had lunch
yet, turn left on North Avenue for two blocks
to The Varsity. A little farther on Peachtree
Street is the Fox Theatre and Road to Tara
Museum.

Between 5th and 10th Streets You will find that
this area is rather seedy and the primary turf
of prostitutes, so you may want to take the train
from the North Avenue station to the Midtown
station (N4), exiting right to Peachtree Street.
Between 10th and 14th Streets are several new
sky-scrapers that rival the Downtown skyline.
Just past 15th Street is the Woodruff Arts
Center, home to the Atlanta Symphony and
Alliance Theater, and next door is the modern
High Museum of Art.

THE SIGHTS

● SciTrek (➤ 39)
● Atlanta Museum (➤ 40)
● NationsBank Plaza Tower
  (➤ 51)
● The Varsity (➤ 63)
● Fox Theatre (➤ 41)
● Road to Tara Museum (➤ 42)
● Woodruff Arts Center
● High Museum of Art (➤ 43)

INFORMATION

Distance 3 miles
Time 40 minutes (no stops); 2–3
hours to take time to view inside
buildings and sights
Start point Midtown (where walk
can be divided)
🚌 F5
✉ Peachtree Street at North
  Avenue
🚆 North Avenue (N3)
End point High Museum of Art
🚌 F3
✉ 1280 Peachtree Street
🚆 Arts Center (N5)

*The Westin Peachtree
Plaza Hotel*

EVENING STROLLS

Beware, most crimes in Atlanta happen at night. On these night strolls, exercise extreme caution and stick to the route advised. If you suspect there may be danger, enter a hotel, store, or restaurant.

INFORMATION

Little Five Points
Distance 1 mile (round trip)
Time 30–45 minutes for both sides of street; longer to browse and window shop
Start point Austin Avenue at Euclid Avenue
➕ J6
🚌 3
End point Euclid Avenue at Moreland Avenue
➕ K5
🚌 3, 48

Downtown
Distance 2 miles
Time 1–2 hours
Start point Upper Alabama Street at Central Avenue
➕ F7
🚇 Five Points (0)
End point MARTA Civic Center (N2)
➕ F5
🚇 Civic Center (N2)

LITTLE FIVE POINTS

Little Five Points is Atlanta's version of New York City's Greenwich Village, a small bohemian quarter with interesting music clubs, restaurants, art galleries, theaters, health food groceries and offbeat shops. It is best seen at night when the clubs are open and its regulars —artists, aging hippies, grunge rockers, and other alternative-culture types—are here in full force. Beginning at Austin and Euclid Avenues, follow Euclid Avenue north to Moreland Avenue and a plaza area where street musicians, mimes, and other performers entertain pedestrians. A few more stores are found off the plaza on Moreland and Seminole Avenues. There are stores on both sides of the street, so repeat the route to avoid crossing back and forth.

DOWNTOWN

Downtown Atlanta is very pretty when lit up at night. From the Upper Alabama Street level at Underground Atlanta (► 29), go to its Central Avenue end and peer across the railing at the State Capitol of Georgia (► 27), The World of Coca-Cola (► 28) with its dramatic pinwheeling neon logo, and the fountain at Depot Plaza. Backtracking, pause to look at the skyscrapers northward, then follow Peachtree Street to Woodruff Park (► 59) for another view of the buildings. Half mile farther on at International Boulevard, turn right down the hill to Courtland Street, turning around for another good view of the skyline. Continue left to Baker Street, then left back up to Peachtree Street, crossing to Hardy Ivy Park, then right on West Peachtree Street to the MARTA Civic Center station. Just beyond the station are good sight lines back up Peachtree and views of the skyscrapers in Midtown.

ORGANIZED SIGHTSEEING

AMERICAN SIGHTSEEING ATLANTA

Runs the following tours: "Atlanta…A City of Winners" which covers the city highlights, and "Homegrown Hits" which goes to CNN, The World of Coca-Cola, and Underground Atlanta. An all-day excursion to Stone Mountain Park includes a skylift trip to the top of the mountain and a cruise on a paddle wheel riverboat.

✉ **550 Pharr Road** ☎ **404/239-9140 or 800/572-3050**

ATLANTA PRESERVATION CENTER

Volunteers lead ten inexpensive walking tours of historic areas and neighborhoods including the Fox Theatre, Sweet Auburn/Martin Luther King, Jr. National Historic District, Druid Hills, Inman Park, Historic Downtown, Ansley Park, Piedmont Park, and Underground Atlanta.

✉ **156 7th Street** ☎ **404/876-2041 or 404/876-2040**

BIRD'S-EYE VIEW

Historic Air Tours ✉ DeKalb–Peachtree Airport, in the suburb of Chamblee (call for correct street entrance: ☎ 770/457-5217) takes visitors high above the city in a private, 4-seater Cessna 172 airplane for a dramatic bird's-eye perspective of the city that focuses primarily on architectural and historic highlights. Its three tours range from 20 to 55 minutes long.

GRAY LINE OF ATLANTA

Provides short tours of Downtown, Midtown, or Buckhead, and a day-long tour that covers Atlanta's primary sights and attractions, plus Stone Mountain and the King Center.

✉ **370 Lee Mill Road, Forest Park** ☎ **404/767-0594**

LOWDER CITY TOURS

Offers thematic tours of Atlanta's historic sites, Stone Mountain Park, Atlanta nightlife, black heritage, and a tour they call "Carter, King, and Coke" for all group sizes (limousine, van, or passenger bus). Tours are between 3 and 8 hours in length.

✉ **131 Ponce de Leon Avenue** ☎ **800/354-1961 or 404/874-1349**

Midtown skyline from Piedmont Park Lake

EXCURSIONS

INFORMATION

Kennesaw Mountain National Battlefield Park
Distance 25 miles north of downtown Atlanta
Time 30–45 minutes
Directions Follow I-75 north to exit 116, Barrett Parkway. Turn left and follow the signs to the Park
➕ Off grid C1
✉ 900 Kennesaw Mountain Drive, Kennesaw, GA 30144
☎ 770/427-4686
🕐 Daily 8:30–5
♿ Free

Roswell
Distance 15 miles north of Buckhead
Time 30–45 minutes
Directions Follow Roswell Road (US 19) north from Peachtree Road in Buckhead until you see the town square (scenic route) or take GA 400 north to the second Northridge Road exit (pass under bridge). Turn right to Roswell Road, then right.
➕ Off grid F1
✉ 617 Atlanta Street, Roswell, GA 30075 (Historic Roswell Convention & Visitors Center)
☎ 404/640-3253
🕐 Mon–Fri 9–5; Sat 10–4; Sun 12–3
🚌 85 from Lenox station (N7)
♿ Free for walking tour; nexpensive for Bulloch Hall

KENNESAW MOUNTAIN NATIONAL BATTLEFIELD PARK

Kennesaw Mountain, located a short distance northwest of Atlanta near Marietta, was an important military objective of the Union Army in 1864, one of the last major barriers before reaching Atlanta. The 2,882-acre park preserves the site of the crucial battle that lasted from June 5 to July 2, pitting 100,000 Union soldiers against 50,000 Confederates. Cannons, monuments, markers, earthworks, and a small museum tell the story of the battle. It also has 16 miles of hiking trails, with a couple of strenuous ascents up the mountain as a contrast to the surrounding flat and rolling terrain.

ROSWELL

The historic suburb of Roswell, located a few miles north of the Chattahoochee River, offers a look at the Old South. Founded in 1839, it managed to survive the onslaught of Sherman's Union Army, who only destroyed the mills that supplied cotton and woolen goods to the Confederate Army. The Roswell Historical Society provides a walking tour of 22 stately mansions and buildings from the 1840s, plus a river crossing, original town square, and three cemeteries. Bulloch Hall (▶ 52) is the only home regularly open to the public.

Kennesaw Mountain National Battlefield Park

Excursions

CHATEAU ÉLAN WINERY

Begun in 1981, Château Élan is Georgia's premier winery and a popular resort spread over 2,400 acres of rolling countryside. Within its main building, a replicated French château, there are tours of the winery with free samples, plus a wine market, gift shop, art gallery, bistro, and formal restaurant. The resort area includes two golf courses, health spa, tennis center, equestrian center, and a conference center. Several annual events, including British Car Day (May) and Bastille Day (July 14), make it a fun place to visit.

Chateau Élan Winery

BRASSTOWN BALD

At 4,874 feet above sea level, Brasstown Bald is the highest point in Georgia, with a panoramic view of the southern Appalachian Mountains. The visitors' center explains the mountain's history and has displays of native plants and wildlife. The mountains here are especially pretty in the spring as wildflowers bloom and in the fall when tree foliage turns to brilliant shades of yellow, orange, and red. En route to this site, you will pass through Helen, a replica of a Bavarian alpine village, and cross the Appalachian Trail, a 2,000-mile hiking trail from Georgia to Maine.

INFORMATION

Chateau Élan Winery
Distance 40 miles northeast of downtown Atlanta
Time 45–60 minutes
Directions Take I-85 north to exit 48 (GA 211) and turn left for a short distance
➕ Off grid G1
✉ 100 Tour de France, Braselton, GA 30075
☎ 800/233-WINE, 770/441-9463
🕐 10–10
💰 Free for winery; admission charge for some festivals

Brasstown Bald
Distance 115 miles north of downtown Atlanta
Time 2 hours
Directions Take I-85 north, diverging left on to I-985. Turn left at GA 52 and right at US 129 to Cleveland. Turn right at GA 75 to Helen and AT trail, left at GA 180, and right at GA 180 spur to Brasstown Bald parking lot
➕ Off grid G1
✉ 1881 Highway 515, Blairsville, GA 30512 (administrator)
☎ 706/896-2555 (visitors' center)
🕐 June 1–Nov 15 10–6, daily; open Apr and May, Sat, Sun only; closed Nov 16–Mar 31
💰 Parking fee

21

WHAT'S ON

Atlanta hosts numerous annual events. Those listed below and others are described in the *Atlanta Journal* and *Atlanta Constitution*'s Friday "Weekend Preview" or Saturday "Leisure" tabloid sections and several other publications (▶93).

JANUARY	King Week remembers Martin Luther King, Jr. through a week-long festival of lectures, films, parades, and musical entertainment.
APRIL	Dogwood Festival is a week-long celebration of spring with concerts, home tours, craft shows, and a balloon race starting at Piedmont Park. Inman Park Festival and Tour of Homes is an excellent opportunity to explore the interiors of the Victorian homes in Atlanta's oldest suburb.
JULY	Independence Day begins with the annual Peachtree Road Race, followed by a parade, and culminates at night with gigantic firework displays. National Black Arts Festival is a week-long celebration of black culture through art exhibits, films, music, and literature.
SEPTEMBER	Arts Festival of Atlanta is held for nine days in Piedmont Park and is the annual event that Atlantans look forward to most. The outdoor event brings some of the best visual artists, crafts people, theater and street performers to the city. The Artist's Market, lining the streets of Piedmont Park, is the main draw, with theatrical and musical entertainment attracting large crowds at night. It begins on the second Saturday in September. Yellow Daisy Festival in Stone Mountain Park features 400 arts and crafts people and entertainment.
OCTOBER	Scottish Festival and Highland Games in Stone Mountain Park attracts over 100 clans for a celebration of dance, music, and traditional games.
NOVEMBER	Lighting of the Great Tree (Atlanta city Christmas tree), accompanied by choirs and musicians, at Underground Atlanta.
DECEMBER	Macy's Eggleston Christmas Parade on Peachtree Street. Festival of Trees displays over 200 Christmas trees decorated by local designers, garden clubs, and schools.

ATLANTA's
top 25 sights

The sights are numbered from south to north across the city

1

ZOO ATLANTA

HIGHLIGHTS

- Willie B
- Ford African Rain Forest
- Sumatran tigers
- Masai Mara
- African elephant show
- Birds of prey demonstration
- Sea lion feedings
- OK-To-Touch Corral
- Sanaga Overlook Aviary
- Reptile feedings

INFORMATION

- H9
- 800 Cherokee Avenue
- 404/624-5678; recorded information 404/624-5600
- Daily 10–4:30; Sat, Sun during Daylight Saving Time 10–5:30 (mid-spring–mid-fall); closed Jan 1, 3rd Mon in Jan, 4th Thu in Nov, Dec 25
- Good café with southern-style meals ($$), several concession stands and snack bars ($)
- Five points (0), then Zoo Trolley (summer months), 31, 32, 97
- Very good
- Expensive
- Cyclorama (➤ 25), Oakland Cemetery (➤ 33)
- Guided group tours. Gift shops, lecture series, workshops, day camps for children, and numerous annual events including night walks and behind-the-scenes visits

Ten years ago, I never went to the city zoo. It was a disgrace, a dirty facility with animals crammed into small and unsanitary cages. Now it has had its $35 million renovation program and I look forward to its next new exhibit.

Wildlife education Spread over 40 acres at Zoo Atlanta are more than 1,000 animals living in natural habitats that replicate the animals' original geographical homes. By each habitat are signs, exhibits, information stations, or video displays to educate visitors about the wildlife and its environment. Regular feedings and entertaining demonstrations offer further insight about the animals.

Lions, tigers, and more Not to be missed are the African habitats of Mzima Springs, an East African watering hole where you'll view several elephants, and Masai Mara, which simulates the expansive Kenya plains with roaming zebras, black rhinoceros, gazelles, and ostriches. From a rock outcrop enclosure, lions overlook the scene. Next door is the lush Ford African Rain Forest, a series of gorilla and monkey environments separated by moats. Among its residents is the zoo mascot Willie B, a male gorilla who finally fathered a child (Kudzu) a few years ago after a decade of trying. Other highlights include Ketambe, a re-created Indonesian tropical rain forest with rare Sumatran tigers and orangutans; Sea Lion Cove, which features underwater viewing of sea lions; Flamingo Lagoon with baby Pink Chilean flamingos; the Reptile House with exotic and slithery creatures from around the world; and the Children's Zoo with an area where they can pet the animals. Future wildlife exhibits include the Okefenokee Swamp/ Georgia Coast with alligators and otters.

CYCLORAMA

When I first looked at it, it was just a big painting. But that all changes as the narration begins. Almost immediately, I became sucked into the sound and fury of the battle, muskets roaring, the screaming of wounded soldiers.

Civil War drama unfolds The Battle of Atlanta, which took place on July 22, 1864, is vividly brought to life at Cyclorama through a circular (358 feet in circumference), 42-foot high, three-dimensional oil painting combined with faux-terrain dioramas that extend 30 feet outward from the painting, plus special sound effects, lighting, music, and narration. The battle is viewed from a slowly revolving seat platform in the inner core of the painting. The 16,000-square foot canvas, painted on Belgian linen, was completed in 1886 by 11 Eastern European artists. Damaged over the years by bacteria, water, insects, rodents and other elements, an $11 million restoration program in the 1970s returned it to its original splendor.

Other attractions The building housing Cyclorama also contains a museum with Civil War artifacts, paintings, photographs, weapons, uniforms, maps, the steam locomotive *Texas*, and a video presentation about the restoration.

HIGHLIGHTS

- Cyclorama painting
- Dioramas
- Multimedia production
- "Life in Camp" display
- Cannons
- Weapons
- Uniforms
- Confederate leader portraits
- Union leader portraits
- Civil War photographs
- *Texas* steam locomotive

INFORMATION

- ✚ H8
- ✉ 800 Cherokee Avenue
- ☎ 404/658-7625; recorded information 404/624-1071
- 🕐 Oct–May, daily 9:30–4:30; Jun–Sep, daily 9:30–5:30; closed Jan 1, 3rd Mon in Jan, 4th Thu in Nov, Dec 25
- 🚇 Five Points (0), then bus 31, 97; or King Memorial (E2), then bus 32
- ♿ Good
- 💲 Moderate
- ↔ Zoo Atlanta (➤ 24), Oakland Cemetery (➤ 33)
- ❓ Cyclorama show every half hour. Gift shop

Cyclorama houses the famous oil painting of the Battle of Atlanta

3

WREN'S NEST

HIGHLIGHTS

- Tar Baby doll
- Uncle Remus character sculptures
- Br'er Fox doll
- Carved wood Br'er Rabbit tobacco holder
- Life-size Uncle Remus diorama
- Japanese edition of *Uncle Remus*
- Harris's typewriter
- Original mailbox
- Gas light fixtures
- "Grumble" box

INFORMATION

- ✚ C8
- ✉ 1050 Ralph David Abernathy Boulevard
- ☎ 404/753-7735; recorded information 404/753-8535
- 🕐 Tue–Sat 10–4; Sun 1–4; closed Jan 1, 4th Thu in Nov, Dec 24–25
- 🚇 West End (S2)
- 🚌 71
- ♿ None
- 💲 Moderate
- ❓ Atlanta Preservation "West End" walking tour (▶ 19). Storytelling every Sat, Wren's Nest Fest (May), Christmas Festival (Dec)

When I was a young child, I was captivated by the Uncle Remus tales featuring Br'er Fox and Tar Baby. It's interesting to see where this author worked, his possessions providing clues to his era and influences.

An author's home The Wren's Nest, an 1870s farm house with a Queen Anne/Victorian façade, was the home of Georgia author and journalist Joel Chandler Harris (1848–1908), who wrote many of the *Uncle Remus* stories from a wicker rocking chair on the wraparound porch. Named after a family of wrens who once nested in his mailbox, it has nine rooms filled with family memorabilia, furnishings and photographs, first edition copies of the *Uncle Remus* tales in several foreign languages, and oddities such as the "Grumble Box," a small wooden box set on the dining room table within which his daughters deposited a coin every time Chandler or his wife caught them complaining.

Creating a classic A slide presentation shows how Chandler began his writing career at the age of 13, as an apprentice—for four years—on a plantation newspaper in central Georgia. It was there, listening to the slaves, that he became enchanted for a lifetime by their African folk tales of talking animals. In 1877, employed as an editorial columnist for the *Atlanta Constitution*, he recalled these tales while thinking about a topic for his next column. With the goal to recapture their spirit, his stories feature a black narrator with the authentic slave dialects.

The tradition of storytelling To perpetuate Chandler's love for storytelling, members of the Southern Order of Storytellers perform every Saturday at 2 P.M.

4

STATE CAPITOL OF GEORGIA

A visit to the State Capitol when the state legislature is in session is especially interesting and entertaining. With a number of flamboyant characters and a helter skelter atmosphere, these sessions often resemble a three-ring circus.

Exterior The neoclassical-styled Georgia State Capitol building, dedicated on July 4, 1889, was Atlanta's first symbol of rebirth from the Civil War. Its shiny, 75 foot-high gold dome, topped by a statue of Liberty, is a city landmark seen from several downtown locations. The double winged building features a majestic entrance, a four-story portico with stairs leading up to the second level, its upper pediment supported by six, two-story-tall Corinthian columns. In the grounds, shaded by large oak and magnolia trees, are state historical markers commemorating the Battle of Atlanta and various statues representing famous Georgians.

Interior The marbled 237 foot-high rotunda is filled with marble busts and portraits of past governors, plus tattered flags from Georgia Civil War regiments. In both wings, hanging from the staircases leading to the legislative chambers, are flags from all 50 states and those that have flown over Georgia, including a British flag and several of the Confederacy. On the fourth floor is the Georgia State Museum of Science and Industry (► 54).

HIGHLIGHTS

- Gold dome
- Main entrance
- Rotunda
- Hall of Flags south wing
- Hall of Flags north wing
- Confederate regiment flags
- Military rifle collection (museum)
- Native American exhibit (museum)
- Two-headed cow (museum)

INFORMATION

- ✚ F7
- ✉ 206 Washington Street
- ☎ 404/656-2000; recorded information 404/656-2844
- 🕑 State Capitol: free guided tours at 10A.M., 11A.M., 1P.M. and 2P.M. Mon–Fri; Georgia State Museum of Science and Industry: Mon–Fri 8:30–5; Sat 10–4; Sun noon–4; closed Jan 1, Easter Mon, last Mon in May, Jul 4, 1st Mon in Sep, 4th Thu in Nov, Dec 24–25
- 🍴 Good cafeteria ($) in building opposite, part of Georgia State (E1) station
- Ⓢ Georgia State (E1)
- 🚌 9, 10, 21, 55, 74, 90, 97
- ♿ Good
- ✚ Free
- ↔ World of Coca-Cola (► 28), Underground Atlanta (► 29), Atlanta Heritage Row (► 30)
- ❓ Indian Heritage Week (2nd week in Nov)

The Hall of Flags

5

THE WORLD OF COCA-COLA

HIGHLIGHTS

- Revolving entrance sign
- Bottling fantasy sculpture
- 1930s soda fountain
- Club Coca-Cola
- Copy of original formula
- Vintage magazine advertisements
- Classic television commercials
- Radio jingles on a 1930s jukebox
- Antique bottling equipment
- Coca-Cola toys

INFORMATION

- ✚ F7
- ✉ 55 Martin Luther King, Jr. Drive
- ☎ Recorded information/voice mail 404/676-5151
- 🕐 Mon–Sat 10–9:30; Sun noon–6; closed Jan 1, 2nd Mon in Jan, Easter Mon, 4th Thu in Nov, Dec 24–25
- 🍴 Coca-Cola product drinks only (free); several restaurants and fast food outlets at nearby Underground Atlanta
- Ⓒ Georgia State (E1), Five Points (0)
- 🚌 4, 9, 10, 17, 49, 74, 90, 97
- ♿ Very good
- 💲 Inexpensive
- ↔ State Capitol of Georgia (➤ 27), Underground Atlanta (➤ 29), Atlanta Heritage Row (➤ 30)
- ❓ Gift shop

Although this museum is just one big advertisement for Coca-Cola—hardly necessary for the world's most popular soft drink—it is worth seeing for its high-tech exhibits and to drink samples of its products sold in other countries.

Atlanta's finest company Served for the first time in 1886 at an Atlanta pharmacy soda fountain, Coca-Cola, its history and its projections for the future are presented at The World of Coca-Cola. After passing beneath a revolving Coca-Cola globe hanging 18 feet above the entrance—a special sight at night with its flashing, pinwheel pattern—you enter a three-story atrium connected to four gallery exhibit areas.

Celebrating a product Gallery One features a futuristic look at the bottling process through a whimsical, kinetic sculpture and over 1,000 pieces of memorabilia from company archives. In the second gallery is a replica of a 1930s soda fountain, and in the third gallery, a high-tech film takes a look at the product's international character. The final gallery shows the drink's

advertising history, including infamous jingles like "Coke is It." Before leaving, stop at Club Coca-Cola, a futuristic soda fountain where you can sip samples of the Coca-Cola products, and also at the Trademart gift shop, which is full of clothing and many souvenirs bearing the Coca-Cola logo.

UNDERGROUND ATLANTA

Beneath Peachtree Street is essentially another city, one that actually existed in the past. Hearing trains passing by it on nearby tracks makes it easy to imagine what the early days of Atlanta might have been like.

On historical ground Underground Atlanta—located a few steps southwest of the point where Atlanta began as a railroad terminus in 1837—is a unique juxtaposition of past history with modern elements. Spanning an extensive area covering six blocks, this entertainment and shopping complex was created by restoring the underground brick streets, ornamental building façades, and tunnels that had fallen into disuse in 1929 after the city built viaducts over the railroad tracks in order to accommodate motorized traffic.

Shopping and sights Underground Atlanta's Upper and Lower Alabama Streets feature specialty stores selling art, books, clothes, regional foods, and souvenirs from the original storefronts. Adding to the constant festival-like atmosphere are street performers and some 50 merchants hawking a variety of merchandise from pushcarts. Also here are the Olympic Experience, an audio-visual presentation and information center about the Olympic Games in Atlanta in July 1996; Atlanta Heritage Row; and Peachtree Fountains Plaza fronting the main entrance with a series of cascading waterfalls and fountains.

Nightlife Kenny's Alley at the lowest level of Underground Atlanta, with its bars and nightspots that offer various comedy acts, music and dancing, was once occupied by saloons and livery stables.

HIGHLIGHTS

- Atlanta Heritage Row
- Olympic Experience
- Peachtree Fountains Plaza
- Kenny's Alley
- Historic building façades
- Pushcart merchants
- Upper Alabama shops
- Lower Alabama shops
- Wall murals
- Live alligators at Dante's Down the Hatch nightclub (► 81)

INFORMATION

- F7
- Between Peachtree Street and Central Avenue at Upper Alabama Street
- 404/523-2311
- Retail shops Mon–Sat 10–9:30; Sun noon–6; restaurants and Kenny's Alley, open midnight–2 A.M.
- Restaurants ($$–$$$) and food court with some 20 fast food vendors ($)
- Five Points (0)
- 3, 4, 9, 13, 17, 20, 31, 42, 49, 90, 97
- Good (call in advance for directions to elevators)
- Free to browse
- Atlanta Heritage Row (► 30), The World of Coca-Cola (► 28)
- Atlanta Preservation walking tour (► 19). "Lighting of the Great Tree" (city Christmas tree), New Year's Eve celebration

7

ATLANTA HERITAGE ROW

HIGHLIGHTS

- Early Native American display
- Re-created railway station
- Battle of Atlanta bomb shelter
- Grady's New South speech
- 1920s trolley car
- Martin Luther King, Jr.'s pulpit
- *Gone with the Wind* premiere video
- Blues and country music
- *People: The Spirit of Atlanta* video
- Delta jet cockpit

INFORMATION

- ✚ F7
- ✉ 55 Upper Alabama Street at Underground Atlanta
- ☎ 404/584-7879
- 🕐 Tue–Sat 10–5; Sun 1–5; closed Jan 1, 4th Thu in Nov, Dec 25
- 🍴 Fast food court and restaurants at Underground Atlanta (➤ 29)
- 🚇 Five Points (0)
- 🚌 3, 4, 9, 13, 17, 20, 31, 42, 49, 90, 97
- ♿ Very good
- 💲 Inexpensive
- ↔ Underground Atlanta (➤ 29), The World of Coca-Cola (➤ 28), State Capitol of Georgia (➤ 27)
- ❓ Occasional special events

Most history museums, with their undistinguished rows of display cases, bore me. It's a shame they are not like Atlanta Heritage Row where you are thrust into the middle of a re-created event. Witnessing it up close makes history come alive—and for a moment I was a part of it.

Reliving history Atlanta Heritage Row is a fascinating multimedia presentation that makes Atlanta's history come alive by putting the viewer directly in the middle of the action. Divided into six historical periods, each section of touchable, lifelike exhibits evolves into the other aided by sound, videos and a time line. When you pass out of Origins (early Native Americans– 1860) into the Civil War (1861–65), you enter a Battle of Atlanta bomb shelter amid rubble and the sounds of cannon fire, backed by narration from the diaries of those who lived during the time.

Historical eras Other themes include Atlanta Resurgens (1865–1895) with journalist Henry Grady's infamous speech advancing his ideas for a New South; Forward Atlanta (1895–1945) with a 1920s trolley car; and Big League City (1945–1974) where you can stand at Martin Luther King, Jr.'s pulpit to experience his famous "I Have a Dream" speech.

International City International City (1974–present) brings the story of Atlanta up to date. Here you can enter the cockpit of a 1970s Delta Airline jet plane backed by sounds from the control tower. The self-guided tour ends with a 15-minute, high-tech, wide screen video called *People: The Spirit of Atlanta*.

CNN CENTER

It's easy to flip on the television and watch the news, but you'll never take it for granted again after visiting the CNN studio. To see the steps (amid chaos) taken to get the news to the viewers is enlightening.

Ted Turner's world CNN Center is the headquarters of the internationally broadcasted Cable News Network and Headline News, two 24-hour all news networks. A 45-minute studio tour begins by riding up the world's longest escalator to an eighth-floor exhibit on Turner's global broadcasting empire. This includes MGM movie stills, a Galaxy 5 satellite replica, exhibits about the Jacques Cousteau and National Geographic programs carried on the TBS cable station, and items from CNN's 1990–91 Gulf War reportage.

The CNN studio From here you get to witness news in the making as reporters scurry to finish stories—while overhead banks of monitors show the latest events breaking from around the world. Editors and producers coordinate the stories as on-the-air personalities prepare to deliver the news.

HIGHLIGHTS

- CNN news room
- MGM movie stills
- Galaxy 5 satellite replica
- TBS sports exhibit
- Jacques Cousteau exhibit
- National Geographic exhibit
- Gulf War reportage exhibit
- *Gone with the Wind* "Oscar" replica
- The Turner Store
- World's longest escalator

INFORMATION

- ✚ F6
- ✉ 1 CNN Center
- ☎ 404/827-2400; recorded information 404/827-2300
- 🕐 Daily 9–5; closed Jan 1, Easter Mon, last Mon in May, Jul 4, 1st Mon in Sep, 4th Thu in Nov, Dec 24–25
- 🍴 Several restaurants ($$) and fast food outlets ($)
- Ⓜ Omni/Dome/GWCC (W1)
- 🚌 1, 11, 18, 86
- ♿ Excellent
- Moderate
- ↔ Omni Coliseum, Georgia World Congress Center and Georgia Dome are next door
- ❓ Visits by guided tour only. Reservations are strongly recommended. Not recommended for children under 6

The world's longest escalator

SWEET AUBURN

HIGHLIGHTS

- Tomb
- Center museum
- King's birthplace
  501 Auburn Avenue
- Fire Station 6 (c 1894),
  Auburn Avenue at Boulevard
- Ebenezer Baptist Church
  (c 1894), 407 Auburn
  Avenue
- African-American Panoramic
  Experience Museum,
  135 Auburn Avenue
- Big Bethel African Methodist
  Episcopal Church (c 1891),
  220 Auburn Avenue

INFORMATION

Avoid at night

- ✛ G6, H6
- ✉ Auburn Avenue from
  Courtland Street to Howell
  Street; 449 Auburn Avenue
  for MLK Center
- ☎ 404/524-1956
- 🕐 Daily summer 9–8,
  otherwise 9–5:30; closed
  Dec 25
- 🍴 Snack area in Center, few
  restaurants ($–$$) on
  Auburn Avenue
- 🚇 King Memorial (E2)
- 🚌 3, 17, 99
- ♿ Good
- 💲 Inexpensive
- ↔ Oakland Cemetery (➤ 33)
- ❓ Daily tours begin at 9:30A.M.
  Atlanta Preservation walking
  tour (➤ 19). King Week
  (2nd week in Jan). At MLK
  Center: gift shop, conferences
  and ongoing lecture series

Seeing how Atlanta has improved race relations in the past two decades, it is hard to imagine that this area was once run solely by blacks and that they were ostracized from the white business community just a few blocks away.

Sweet Auburn The influence of African-Americans who comprise more than 60 percent of Atlanta's population has been felt most along Auburn Avenue. This district connected to Downtown was from 1890 to 1930 the most prosperous center of black business, entertainment, and political life. Prevented from participating in the white business community, black Atlantans came here to open businesses, attend church and fraternal organizations, and to party.

Martin Luther King, Jr. National Historic District At its east end is the Martin Luther King, Jr. National Historic District, established by the National Park Service in 1980 to preserve the birthplace and boyhood surroundings of the nation's most renowned Civil Rights leader. In the courtyard of the Martin Luther King, Jr. Center for Non-Violent Social Change is King's raised white marble tomb set in the middle of a

"meditation" pool with the inscription "Free at last". The Center's museum contains King's Nobel Peace ' Prize, Bible, typewriter, and many photographs that chronicle the Civil Rights movement.

The birthplace of Martin Luther King, Jr.

OAKLAND CEMETERY

This cemetery reminds me of those found in Europe, not just a burial plot, but a treasure trove of art and history. Along its hilly paths, shaded by massive oak trees, are elaborately decorated burial markers, monuments, and fountains.

A Who's Who of deceased Atlantans Oakland Cemetery, the city's oldest burial ground, contains a mixed assortment of Atlanta citizens. Opened in 1850, it was the only municipal cemetery in Atlanta until 1884. Among its 100,000 occupants are rich and poor, black and white, Jews, and a host of celebrities, including the modest graves of *Gone with the Wind* author Margaret Mitchell (Marsh), Inman Park developer Joel Hurt (► 34) and famed 1930s golfer Bobby Jones, plus 23 Atlanta mayors, six Georgia governors, and five Confederate generals.

Graveyard art Listed on the National Register of Historic Places, the still-used 88-acre cemetery has an incredible collection of Gothic and Classic Revival mausoleums decorated with beautiful stained glass, flamboyant Gothic accents, and sculpture. Made from cast iron, bronze, or stone, they are exquisite examples of artistic craftsmanship, often depicting symbolic Christian metaphors like crosses, swords, lions, and angels.

Battle of Atlanta section From its highest hill, Confederate Commander-in-Chief General John B. Hood surveyed his troops during the Battle of Atlanta. The Confederate Army section, marked by a striking monument of a wounded lion, contains nearly 3,000 soldiers buried shortly after the battle by women and children (► 55).

HIGHLIGHTS

- Jasper Newton Smith statue/mausoleum
- Austell mausoleum
- Marion Kiser mausoleum
- E. W. Marsh mausoleum
- Konz family "Egyptian-style" monument
- "Weeping Woman" statue
- Maurine Robbins tomb
- Neal family monument
- William Allen Fuller monument
- "Children Out in the Rain" fountain

INFORMATION

Avoid at night

- ✚ G7, H7
- ✉ 248 Oakland Avenue
- ☎ 404/688-2107
- ◷ Daily 8–6
- Ⓖ King Memorial (E2)
- 🚌 9, 18, 32
- ♿ None
- 🚻 Free; walking tour brochure available at cemetery office (modest price)
- ↔ MLK Center for Non-Violent Social Change (► 32), Cyclorama (► 25), Zoo Atlanta (► 24)
- ❓ Tours Sat 11A.M., Sun 2P.M. (May–Oct only) for groups of 10–30 by appointment. Annual "Sunday in the Park" festival (Oct)

INMAN PARK

The 19th-century Victorian homes of Inman Park are not to be viewed in a hurry. I often find myself staring at a house, closely examining every turret, fish scale shingle, gable, balcony, fancy molding, and ornate feature.

Atlanta's first suburb Developed in the 1880s by Joel Hurt, the Inman Park neighborhood—located east of downtown Atlanta near the site of a crucial Civil War battle—was Atlanta's first suburb. Connected to the commercial district by one of the nation's first electric streetcar systems, it swiftly became Atlanta's most prestigious address, attracting city élite such as Coca-Cola founder Asa G. Candler who owned Callan Castle, a huge Greek Revival-style mansion. Hurt owned two homes here, a modest cottage and a large half-Italianate, half-Victorian-styled mansion. He named the neighborhood after his friend Samuel M. Inman.

20th-century changes By 1910, Inman Park began losing residents to newer developed

neighborhoods and became more middle class as lots were subdivided for smaller homes. After World War II, the area went into decline, only to be rediscovered in the 1970s by young professionals who have restored more than 100 neglected homes to their original splendor.

A mansion on Inman Park

HIGHLIGHTS

- Callan Castle (1903), 145 Elizabeth Street
- Hurt Cottage (1882), 117 Elizabeth Street
- Hurt Mansion (1904), 167 Elizabeth Street
- Beath-Dickey House (1898), 866 Euclid Avenue
- Woodruff-Burruss House (1890), 882 Euclid Avenue
- Charles R. Winship House (1893), 814 Edgewood Avenue
- George E. King House (1889), 889 Edgewood Avenue
- Charles V. Lecraw House (1890), 897 Edgewood Avenue

INFORMATION

- J6
- Primarily Edgewood and Euclid Avenues, Hurt and Elizabeth Streets
- Good restaurant ($) opposite Inman Park–Reynoldstown station; others in nearby Little Five Points (▶18)
- Inman Park–Reynoldstown (E3)
- 3, 7, 17, 34, 48, 107
- None
- Little Five Points (▶18), Carter Presidential Center (▶35)
- Atlanta Preservation walking tour (▶19). Inman Park Festival and Tour of Homes (Apr)

CARTER PRESIDENTIAL CENTER & LIBRARY

Although I have been to Washington, D.C., I find this Center offers the best chance to get a close look at the life of a President. Through high-tech interactive videos, you can even talk to President Carter about issues in his administration.

The Carter Presidential Center and Library is located on historic "Copenhill." At this vantage point, which overlooks downtown Atlanta, General Sherman watched the raging battle from the Augustus Hurt House.

Understated exterior The Center consists of four austere, circular buildings. You approach it along a winding driveway lined with flags from many nations, to a central fountained pool and double colonnaded entryway. Behind the Center, a Japanese garden, with beautiful flowers, shrubbery, and a man-made stream, lake, and waterfall, is a serene spot to relax in, with the Atlanta skyline in the background.

Carter Library Museum The exhibits in the Carter Library Museum use documents, furniture, clothes, and family mementos to celebrate Jimmy Carter's life from his beginnings as a peanut farmer in central Georgia, to becoming a naval officer, state senator, Georgia governor, U.S. President, and humanitarian. Planned as a complete learning facility, the museum also examines the presidency in general, with a film and temporary exhibits that portray various historical aspects of the presidency. The Center's library, for use by appointment, can be viewed from the museum through a glass partition. It contains over 27 million pages of documents, 1.5 million photographs, and hours of audio and videotapes.

HIGHLIGHTS

- Re-created Oval Office
- Carter's early years exhibit
- Presidential issues exhibit
- Japanese garden
- Gifts from foreign leaders
- Town Meeting exhibit
- 1976 Presidential campaign memorabilia
- Presidential history film
- State dinner table setting replica
- Interactive "Carter" videos

INFORMATION

- ⊞ J5
- ✉ 1 Copenhill Avenue
- ☎ 404/331-3942; recorded information 404/331-0296
- 🕐 Mon–Sat 9–4:45; Sun noon–4:45; closed Jan 1, 4th Thu in Nov, Dec 25
- 🍴 Good cafeteria ($); open Mon–Sat 11–4; Sun noon–4:30
- Ⓜ Inman Park–Reynoldstown (E3)
- 🚌 2, 16
- ♿ Very good
- 💲 Moderate; children under 16 free
- ↔ Inman Park (▶34), Little Five Points (▶18)
- ❓ Group tours. Temporary art and history exhibits; conferences by invitation only

13

FERNBANK MUSEUM OF NATURAL HISTORY

HIGHLIGHTS

- IMAX Theater
- A Walk Through Time in Georgia
- Dinosaur Hall
- Okefenokee Swamp exhibit
- Spectrum of the Senses
- The World of Shells
- Living Coral Reef & Tropical Fish Aquarium
- DNA model
- Rose gardens (outside)
- Fossil floor

INFORMATION

- ✚ Off grid K4
- ✉ 767 Clifton Road
- ☎ 404/378-0127; recorded information 404/370-0960; IMAX shows 404/370-0019; directions hot line 404/370-0850
- 🕐 Mon–Thu, Sat 10–5; Fri 10–9; Sun noon–5; closed Dec 25
- 🍴 Good dining room with light meals and snacks ($)
- 🚌 North Avenue (N3), then bus 2
- ♿ Good (museum), IMAX (call for special arrangements)
- 🎫 Moderate (museum or IMAX only); very expensive ("combination" ticket)
- ↔ Fernbank Science Center (►37), Michael C. Carlos Museum (►48)
- ❓ Gift shop, occasional workshops, lectures

When here, splurge on a film at the museum's IMAX Theater. From national parks to the Rolling Stones rock band, it's an overwhelming experience to see nature and people presented larger than life on its 52 by 70 foot screen.

The best in the South The Fernbank Museum maintains the largest natural history collection south of the Smithsonian Institution. Set within the 65-acre Fernbank Forest, this modern building with a soaring 85-foot-high entrance atrium and fossils embedded into its limestone floor, features over 150,000 square feet of exhibition space that uses hands-on exhibits, interactive videos, and modern technology to explain the universe.

Popular exhibits Its most popular permanent exhibit, *A Walk Through Time in Georgia*, divides the state into six landform regions to explain how it developed over time. Utilizing large murals and dioramas, its best exhibits are Dinosaur Hall with seven life-size creatures, and the Okefenokee Swamp which re-creates the sights and sounds of this mysterious swamp.

Other exhibits include the Spectrum of the Senses, The World of Shells, a decorative arts collection, and two hands-on Discovery Rooms for children. Fernbank also hosts some of the best exhibitions in North America.

A dinosaur skeleton found in the Gobi Desert, China

14

FERNBANK SCIENCE CENTER

On clear nights when specific planets or other celestial bodies are visible, I, with other Atlantans, head for the Science Center Observatory where the public is allowed to see them up close through its 36-inch reflecting telescope.

Education and entertainment Fernbank Science Center is the only museum in the United States owned and operated by a county school system. This small museum offers entertaining and educational exhibits focusing on ecology, geology, wildlife, space exploration, and modern technology. It has a meteor exhibit, the largest collection of Georgia tektites in the world, an authentic Apollo command module space capsule, a taxidermy reconstruction of a saber-toothed tiger, dioramas of insects, a vanishing wildlife habitats exhibit, and a rock and precious stone collection. As the predecessor of the newer and more elaborate Fernbank Museum of Natural History (►36), there is some overlap of subject matter, including Okefenokee Swamp and dinosaur exhibits.

Planetarium The Center's planetarium, seating 500 people, is the largest in the southeast United States. With a 70 foot projection dome, it features an amazing show of more than 9,000 stars and planets.

Nature trail The two-mile paved nature trail through the adjoining Fernbank Forest offers a bit of peace and calm amid the bustle of the busy city, as no recreational activities or picnics are allowed here. Fernbank Forest is an area of virgin woodland preserved by Emily Harrison, whose father, Colonel Z. Harrison, bought the land in 1881.

HIGHLIGHTS

- Observatory telescope
- Planetarium
- Okefenokee Swamp exhibit
- Dinosaurs
- Apollo space capsule
- Saber-toothed tiger
- Insect exhibits
- Rock and precious stone collection
- Fernbank Forest nature trails
- Georgia tektites collection

INFORMATION

- ✚ Off grid K4
- ✉ 156 Heaton Park Drive
- ☎ 404/378-4311; recorded information 404/378-4314, ext. 811 (general), ext. 818 (planetarium shows), ext. 831 (astronomical events)
- ◴ Mon 8:30–5; Tue–Fri 8:30–10; Sat 10–5; Sun 1–5. Extended vacation closings coincide with school system; call in advance
- ▣ North Avenue (N3), then bus 2; or Edgewood–Candler Park (E4), then bus 12
- ♿ Good
- ▣ Free for museum; planetarium inexpensive
- ↔ Michael C Carlos Museum (►48), Fernbank Museum of Natural History (►36)
- ? Laboratory tours during open houses. Gift shop, workshops, lectures, films, open houses, and planetarium showings

15

STONE MOUNTAIN PARK

INFORMATION

- ✚ Off grid F4
- ✉ East on US 78 (look for exit signs)
- ☎ 770/498-5600
- 🕐 Daily 6–midnight; closed Dec 25
- 🍴 Several restaurants ($$) and food concessions ($) throughout the park
- 🚇 Avondale (E7), then bus 120
- ♿ Good at most attractions
- 🎫 Moderate park entrance fee (per car); expensive combination attractions ticket
- ❓ Regular festivals

On a clear day, the best view of the Atlanta metropolitan area is seen from atop Stone Mountain, an observation post used in past centuries by Native Americans, surveyors, and Civil War troops. I wonder if they too were awestruck by the view, especially the spectacular sunsets seen from here.

Stone Mountain Park, Georgia's number one tourist attraction, offers a cornucopia of things to see and do.

Confederate Memorial carving Prominently seen from many Atlanta locations, Stone Mountain is the world's largest exposed granite outcropping (825 feet high). It is even more famous for the Confederate Memorial bas-relief sculpture carved into its rock face, a 90-foot-high by 190-foot-wide likeness of Confederate leaders Jefferson Davis, Robert E. Lee, and Stonewall Jackson on their horses.

Laser light show From April to November, the lawn beneath the sculpture is packed every night with people watching the spectacular laser light show cast on the mountain face. The top of the mountain can be reached by following a one and a quarter mile trail or by skylift.

Other attractions A combined historical display and recreational site, the 3,200-acre park also contains a reassembled, 19-building *ante bellum* plantation brought here from other Georgia locations, a steam locomotive ride around the mountain's five-mile diameter base, an antique auto and musical instruments museum, Civil War exhibits, two golf courses, beach, lake, zoo, campground, and paddle-wheel riverboat.

SCITREK

I hate museums where it is just look and don't touch. At SciTrek, the exhibits require hands-on participation. It's a great place for the curious of all ages, where learning scientific principles is turned into a fun activity .

Hands-on museum SciTrek, rated one of the top ten physical science museums in the United States, has more than 100 exhibits illustrating scientific principles through technology. In the Mechanics and Simple Machines exhibition hall, you can lift a real car engine with a basic pulley and gear system, or use a Bernoulli blower to suspend a ball in the air, plus there's a 44-foot-high Eiffel Tower replica made from 18,762 metal "Erector" set pieces. In the Light and Perception section, you can become a human kaleidoscope, or freeze your shadow on a wall covered with light sensitive film. The highlight of the Electricity and Magnetism exhibition is a Van de Graaf generator, which makes your hair stand straight up by producing high-voltage static electricity. In Mathematica, the achievements of mathematicians from the 12th century to the present day are displayed on a wall, and there are various exhibits demonstrating the laws of maths.

Travelling shows and young children A fifth exhibition hall is reserved for traveling technology shows such as electric cars. The Kidspace section is for children ages 2–7, where they learn about the principles of science through play.

HIGHLIGHTS

- Plasma Walk
- Eiffel Tower replica
- Distortion room
- Van de Graaf generator
- Frozen shadow room
- Human gyroscope
- Benham's "color" Disc
- Light Island
- Bernoulli blower
- Impact! gamelike video

INFORMATION

- ✚ G5
- ✉ 395 Piedmont Avenue
- ☎ Recorded information/voice mail 404/522-5500
- 🕐 Mon–Sat 10–5; Sun noon–5; closed Jan 1, Easter Mon, 4th Thu in Nov, Dec 25
- 🍴 Small food concession
- 🚇 Civic Center (N2)
- 🚌 16, 31, 46
- ♿ Very good
- 💲 Expensive
- ↔ Atlanta Museum (➤40)
- ❓ Temporary exhibit tours. Gift shop, summer film festival, workshops, and family programs in conjunction with temporary exhibitions

An electrical demonstration with Jacob's Ladder

17

ATLANTA MUSEUM

HIGHLIGHTS

- Civil War rifles
- Japanese Zero airplane
- Napoleon's hair
- World War I cannon
- Davy Crockett's rifle
- Adolf Hitler's cigar box
- General Custer's hairbrush
- Queen Victoria's shawl
- Margaret Mitchell's armchair
- President Franklin D. Roosevelt's urinary jar

INFORMATION

- F5
- 537 Peachtree Street
- 404/872-8233
- Mon–Fri 10–5; by appointment for groups (20+; weekends only)
- Two excellent restaurants ($$) a half block north
- North Avenue (N3)
- 2, 10, 27, 31
- None
- Inexpensive
- Road to Tara Museum (► 42), Fox Theatre (► 41), SciTrek (► 39)
- Antiques shop on first floor

This is the oddest museum in Atlanta. A visit here is more like browsing through the attic of an eccentric old relative who collected anything that struck their fancy, a hoarder's paradise that's both interesting and weird.

History of a collector The Atlanta Museum, housed on the second floor of a 25-room, red-brick Victorian-style house built in 1900 for wealthy distillery owner Rufus M. Rose, founder of the Four Roses Distillery, is the private collection of J. H. Elliott. It contains an eclectic assortment of over 2,500 historical objects, most of which have nothing to do with Atlanta. Beginning as a teenager in 1899 with Indian artifacts, Elliott moved into full gear when he entered the antiques business in 1923. Running out of room for his business and collection, he moved into the Rufus Rose House in 1945. His antiques business, now run by his son and grandson, still occupies the first floor of the house.

An eclectic collection Although there are designated Margaret Mitchell and Civil War rooms, the latter having an especially good collection of weapons and uniform accessories, the collection's jumbled arrangement defies good organization. A case holding a stone and vase from King Tut's tomb sits beside a lock of Napoleon's hair and a tablecloth belonging to Lafayette. Look for Adolf Hitler's cigar box, General Custer's hairbrush, Davy Crockett's rifle, and Queen Victoria's shawl. From a World War I cannon to a Japanese Zero airplane, there's so much crammed into this museum, that you have to circle through its rooms more than once to make sure you've seen everything.

FOX THEATRE

I never get tired of the Fox Theatre, nor does it cease to amaze me. Like a madcap dream turned into reality, its interior and exterior are truly works of art. Before a show, arrive early so you can investigate every nook and cranny.

History preserved The glamorous Fox Theatre, still used for Broadway shows, rock concerts, dance performances, and film festivals, is one of only a few classic movie palaces left in the United States. It was built in 1929 in a fabulous Moorish-Egyptian style to be the headquarters for Atlanta's Arabic Order of the Nobles of the Mystic Shrine (a Masonic order). When they ran into financial difficulty, it was purchased by movie mogul William Fox, who turned it into a theater. In 1978, facing destruction from the corporation who bought it, it was saved from the wrecking ball by a local preservation group.

Architecturally unique With walls of alternating cream and buff colored brick, its exterior features three copper-clad onion domes, watch towers, lancet arches, machicolated walls, and a huge bronze marquee over the entrance. Once inside the 4,518-seat auditorium, look upward at the mystical "sky" ceiling complete with softly floating clouds and twinkling stars that can be transformed into a morning or evening sky. Accented by minarets and castellated walls, it's like sitting in the courtyard of an Arabian palace.

HIGHLIGHTS

- Sky ceiling
- Marquee at night
- Moorish-designed side entrance
- Egyptian ballroom
- Brass trimmed ticket booths
- Möller organ (3,622 pipes)
- Dress circle promenade
- Men's and women's lounges
- Terrazzo-tile floors
- Sequinned stage curtain design

INFORMATION

- F4
- 660 Peachtree Street
- 404/881-2100; recorded information 404/876-2040
- Determined by event
- Concession stand during events; good restaurant next door and opposite ($$)
- North Avenue (N3)
- 2, 10, 13, 27, 31, 45, 99
- Good
- Expensive (tours)
- Road to Tara Museum (➤42), Atlanta Museum (➤40)
- Atlanta Preservation Walking tour (➤19)

ROAD TO TARA MUSEUM

HIGHLIGHTS

- Film clips
- Original posters
- Costume Gallery
- Movie props
- Autographed *Gone with the Wind* first editions
- Actor/actress photographs
- Doll Gallery
- Civil War exhibit
- Original costume sketches
- Foreign *Gone with the Wind* editions

INFORMATION

- ✚ F4
- ✉ 659 Peachtree Street
- ☎ 404/897-1939
- 🕐 Mon–Sat 10–6; Sun 1–6; closed Dec 25
- 🍴 Good restaurant next door and opposite ($$)
- Ⓟ North Avenue (N3)
- 🚌 2, 10, 13, 27, 31, 45, 99
- ♿ Good
- 💲 Moderate (tours)
- ↔ Fox Theatre (➤41), Atlanta Museum (➤40)
- ❓ Tour by prearranged appointment. Gift shop, occasional lectures, seminars

Visitors to Atlanta have asked me where Tara, the ante bellum *mansion from* Gone with the Wind, *is located. Unfortunately, it doesn't exist. The only place to re-live that romantic tale is at the Road to Tara Museum.*

Truth and fiction The Road to Tara Museum, named after Margaret Mitchell's original title for the famed novel, houses an impressive collection of *Gone with the Wind* memorabilia that allows visitors to rediscover the Civil War from both a real and fictional viewpoint. It also offers an in-depth look at Margaret Mitchell's life with film clips, personal letters, and photographs.

A classic movie Views of the movie, from its making to the completed product, are presented in three galleries. The main gallery has original posters, murals, and photographs to reacquaint you with the movie's characters; the Costume Gallery has reproductions of the clothes worn by the cast; and the Doll Gallery features over 100 different *Gone with the Wind* character dolls created from 1937 to 1992. A film on the making of the movie is shown in the David O. Selznick Screening Room.

Historic location The former luxury Georgian Terrace Hotel, in which the museum is housed, was the place where Margaret Mitchell first presented her completed manuscript to her publisher and where the cast stayed for the 1939 Atlanta première.

Some members of the movie cast

HIGH MUSEUM OF ART

The High Museum is a sight to behold both inside and out. Its bright white walls and vast sky-lit atrium create a light and airy atmosphere that makes it seem more like a garden than a museum, and ensures a pleasurable environment to view art.

Post-Modern architecture The High Museum of Art, its exterior walls covered with white porcelain-enameled steel panels, is an innovative building that receives more raves for its architecture than its art collection. Built in 1983 by premier American architect Richard Meier, it resembles a giant cubist-geometric sculpture dropped on the lawn. From the pavement, a slanted entrance ramp leads upward to a three-story, bowed glass window that looks into a sky-lit atrium. A lobby to the right shaped like a grand piano juts outward and a blocky, semi-detached auditorium building set at a 45-degree angle to the left completes the building's look from the street. Inside, galleries on all levels radiate in a semi-circular manner off the atrium.

Permanent collection The High Museum excels in American decorative arts, sub-Saharan African art, 19th-century American landscapes, American post-World War II modern works, and its Uhry Print Collection, which contains works by notable French Impressionists, Post-Impressionists, German Expressionists, and post-war American modern artists. It also has the obligatory Rodin sculpture and a large Alexander Calder mobile graces the front lawn.

Temporary exhibits Temporary exhibits featuring major artists are held here every month.

HIGHLIGHTS

- *Houses of Parliament*, Claude Monet
- *Marilyn*, Andy Warhol
- *Beach at Sainte-Adresse*, Frédéric Bazille
- *Supreme Hardware Store*, Richard Estes
- *Pow!*, Roy Lichenstein
- *Hayrick*, John Henry Twachtman
- *Descent Into Hell*, Albrecht Dürer
- *Venus*, Vincenzo Catena
- Teke mask from Zaire

INFORMATION

- ✚ F3
- ✉ 1280 Peachtree Street
- ☎ 404/733-4400; recorded information 404/733-HIGH
- 🕐 Tue–Thu 10–5; Fri 10–9; Sat 10–5; Sun noon–5; closed Jan 1, Easter Mon, last Mon in May, Jul 4, 1st Mon in Sep, 4th Thu in Nov, Dec 24–25
- 🍴 Drinks/pastries handcart in atrium ($), good restaurant next door ($$), several restaurants in nearby Colony Square office complex
- 🚇 Arts Center (N5)
- 🚌 10, 23, 35, 36, 98, 148
- ♿ Excellent
- 💲 Moderate (special exhibits often have an additional charge); free on Thu after 1 P.M.
- ↔ Center of Puppetry Arts (▶45), Atlanta Botanical Garden (▶44)
- ❓ Special exhibit tours. Gift shop

43

ATLANTA BOTANICAL GARDEN

HIGHLIGHTS

- Rooster topiary creation
- Poison-arrow frogs display
- Vanilla orchid vine on cacao tree
- Storza Woods
- Waterfall in conservatory
- Double coconut seed (largest in plant kingdom)
- "Living Stones" desert plants
- Japanese Garden
- Lily pond stone carvings
- Carnivorous plant bog

INFORMATION

- ✚ G3
- ✉ 1345 Piedmont Avenue
- ☎ Recorded information/voice mail 404/876-5859
- ◔ Oct–Mar, Tue–Sun 9–6; Apr–Sep, Tue–Sun 9–7; closed Jan 1, Easter Mon, Jul 4, 4th Thu in Nov, Dec 24–25
- 🍴 Lunch cart (Apr–Oct only; $), restaurants, fast food outlets and restaurants half mile away at Ansley Mall
- 🚇 Arts Center (N5)
- 🚌 31, 36
- ♿ Few
- 💲 Moderate; free on Thu after 1 P.M.
- ↔ Piedmont Park (►59), High Museum of Art (►43)
- ❓ Audio tape tour in five languages; special exhibit tours. Gift shop, classes, workshops, and plant sales; library

The Atlanta Botanical Garden is my oasis in this busy city. I love hiking in its woods, looking at the flowers that change with the seasons, and wandering through the many different natural environments found in its conservatory.

The Atlanta Botanical Garden is composed of three separate areas: landscaped gardens, virgin forest, and a conservatory.

The gardens The landscaped outdoor gardens, spread over 15 acres of land, exhibit more than 3,000 different plants, including a rose garden, traditional Japanese garden with bridge and goldfish pond, English herb garden, southern vegetable garden, dwarf and rare conifer garden, fragrance garden for the blind, and a rock garden.

Storza Woods The Storza Woods is a 15-acre preserved hardwood forest with paved trails where you can view plants native to Georgia in their natural setting. An especially beautiful area from April to June when native Georgian flowering shrubs and trees are in full bloom, its "Upper Woodland" section features a backyard wildlife habitat and a fern glade with recycling stream.

Dorothy Chapman Fuqua Conservatory Plants from various desert and tropical environments,

plus endangered plant species, are grown within this fascinating environment that is controlled by a computer. Huge leaves provide a canopy over walkways enhanced by splashing waterfalls and chirping birds.

CENTER OF PUPPETRY ARTS

Puppetry is not just for children. After a visit here, I discovered that it is a sophisticated and interesting form of entertainment that requires craftsmanship, mechanical ability, and acting skill. Above all, it made me laugh.

The Center of Puppetry Arts is one of only two facilities in the United States specializing in this Old World entertainment medium and art form. Since opening in 1978, it has expanded public awareness about puppetry through a variety of educational and entertainment programs.

Education The history and use of puppets is best explained at the Center's International Puppet Museum, a fascinating collection of over 200 hand, string, rod, and shadow puppets that span several centuries and cultures. It includes miniature pre-Columbian clay puppets, ritualistic African figures, Punch and Judy from France, and the Muppets, America's most beloved puppets featuring Kermit the Frog and Miss Piggy. PuppetWorks, a hands-on exhibit, allows visitors to operate similar puppets and the Animatronics display introduces visitors to new technologies via radio-controlled puppets.

Entertainment With four theaters — up-close and intimate to a 300-seater — puppetry theater is presented regularly by black-clothed professional puppeteers who might use rod puppets, full body puppets, hand puppets, or the classic marionette. Classic tales such as *Pinocchio* and *Cinderella* hold your children spellbound, while Shakespearian dramas, the New Directions series, and Xperimental Puppetry Theater present adult themes. A behind-the-scenes look at the puppeteers is included in some programs.

HIGHLIGHTS

- Live puppet theater
- Kermit the Frog muppet
- Pigs in Space muppets
- Jim Henson (Muppet creator) tribute exhibit
- Trash Phoenix
- PuppetWorks
- Puppet Storeroom
- German scarf puppet
- Punch and Judy
- Animatronics

INFORMATION

- ➕ F3
- ✉ 1404 Spring Street at 16th Street
- ☎ 404/873-3391; recorded information 404/874-0398
- 🕐 Mon–Sat 9–4 for museum; varies for performances; closed Jan 1, Easter Mon, last Mon in May, Jul 4, 1st Mon in Sep, 4th Thu in Nov, Dec 24–25
- 🚇 Arts Center (N5)
- ♿ Good
- 💲 Inexpensive for museum; moderate for performances
- ❓ High Museum of Art (➤ 43) Gift shop, regular workshops

23

ATLANTA HISTORY CENTER

HIGHLIGHTS

- Swan House
- Civil War collection
- Tullie Smith Farm
- Battle of Atlanta exhibit
- Folk life exhibit
- *Gone with the Wind* gallery
- Costume collection
- Swan Woods Trail
- Asian-American Gardens
- Farm animals

INFORMATION

- ⊞ Off grid F1
- ✉ 130 West Paces Ferry Road
- ☎ 404/814-4000; recorded information on this line after closing hours
- 🕐 Mon–Sat 10–5:30; Sun noon–5; closed Jan 1, 4th Thu in Nov, Dec 24–25
- 🍴 Good cafe ($) in museum and restaurant ($) near Swan House
- 🚇 Lenox (N7), then bus 23; or Lindbergh (N6), then bus 40; or West Lake (W4), then bus 58
- ♿ Few
- 💲 Expensive
- ↔ Georgia Governor's Mansion (➤47), Buckhead (➤58)
- ❓ Swan House tours. Regular series of lectures, workshops, programs, festivals, and annual events such as Civil War Encampment weekend

The Tullie Smith farmhouse

The best way I have found to enjoy this Center is to take it in small chunks. It is just too much visual stimulation to cram into one day, much less fully understand what you have seen. Among its many sights, my favorite is the Swan House.

In the prestigious Buckhead neighborhood is the Atlanta History Center, a 32-acre complex dedicated to preserving, protecting and displaying the history of Atlanta.

History retold The Museum of Atlanta History, opened in 1993, is an awesome collection of documents, clothes, and artifacts that honors Atlanta's heritage since 1835. The permanent exhibition tells Atlanta's complete history, with separate galleries devoted to specific events. The Civil War gallery has nearly 26,000 items, including 800 weapons. Next door in McElreath Hall are the center's archives and library, and an exhibition devoted to the Battle of Atlanta.

Contrasting homes Also on the 32-acre site is Swan House, a classical-style mansion designed by noted architect Philip Shutze in 1926 and owned by a rich cotton broker. Inside, the house is a veritable museum of decorative arts. The

Tullie Smith Farm, a two-story farm house (1845) with outbuildings brought here from another Atlanta location, features barnyard animals and farm life demonstrations. Seven interconnecting gardens and hiking trails make up the rest of the grounds.

24

GEORGIA GOVERNOR'S MANSION

The Georgia governor's mansion, wrapped by a white Doric column portico, reminds me of the plantation houses found in the rural South. I can easily imagine Rhett Butler coming here to sweep Scarlett off her feet.

Exterior The Georgia governor's mansion, completed in 1968 and set in sprawling grounds with many formal flower and shrubbery gardens, is the official residence of the Governor of Georgia. The 24,000 square foot, two-story Greek Revival-styled house—located on top of a hill in the middle of an 18-acre plot—is similar to the first Governor's mansion built in Milledgeville (central Georgia) in 1838, and more closely resembles a Mississippi plantation house than a Georgian *ante bellum* mansion. The red-brick rectangular shape is completely wrapped by a white Doric-columned portico, with its front entrance based on a 1930s design by Asher Benjamin.

Current furnishings Inside the mansion, its beautiful 19th-century furnishings, paintings, and porcelain, including one of the finest collections of Federal Period furniture in the United States, reflect the formality and grandeur of the office. A large bronze state seal inlaid in the white marble floor dominates the entrance to the mansion. Since the furnishings are valuable, tour visitors are not allowed in the actual rooms, but must stand at roped entrances to them while a guide explains the historical significance of each item. The tour includes all the rooms of the first floor, plus the Circular Hall decorated with an early 19th-century Italian chandelier, a full-length portrait of George Washington, and a rare French vase with a portrait medallion of Benjamin Franklin on it.

HIGHLIGHTS

- Benjamin Franklin vase
- George Washington portrait
- Georgia-made huntboard (family dining room)
- Italian chandelier
- Alcove bed (guest bedroom)
- Scroll arm sofas (family living room)
- Silver service (state dining room)
- Library
- Front entrance (exterior)
- Chinese glass paintings (family living room)

INFORMATION

- ✚ Off grid F1
- ✉ 391 West Paces Ferry Road
- ☎ 404/261-1776; recorded information 404/261-1858
- ◷ See tours below
- ◻ Dozens of restaurants in nearby Buckhead business area
- ◻ Lenox (N7), then bus 23; or Lindbergh (N6), then bus 40; or West Lake (W4), then bus 58
- ♿ Very good
- ◻ Free
- ↔ Atlanta History Center (▶46), Buckhead (▶58)
- ❓ Guided tours Tue–Thu 10–11:30; candlelight tours during Christmas season. Reservations required for groups over 20

MICHAEL C. CARLOS MUSEUM

HIGHLIGHTS

- Egyptian mummies
- Floor stencils
- Pre-Columbian collection
- Roman coins
- Re-created Jericho excavation site
- Native American exhibit
- Cuneiform tablets
- Plaster recreations of ancient architectural details
- "Goddess of the West" coffin painting

INFORMATION

- Off grid K2
- 571 Kilgo Street at Emory University
- Recorded information/voice mail 404/727-4282
- Mon–Thu, Sat 10–5; Fri 10–9; Sun noon–5; closed Jan 1, Easter Mon, last Mon in May, Jul 4, 1st Mon in Sep, 4th Thu in Nov, Dec 24–25
- Good restaurant on upper level ($$)
- Edgewood–Candler Park (E4), then bus 6; or Arts Center (N5), then bus 36
- Good
- Free; suggested donation
- Fernbank Science Center (►37), Fernbank Museum of Natural History (►36)
- Group tours. Gift shop, annual Before Christ Fest, regular lectures, films, workshops, and special traveling exhibitions

While you're looking up, also look down. On the floor are stenciled diagrams that help you understand the exhibit item's place in history. It may be the floor plan of an ancient mortuary temple or the meandering course of the Nile River.

Post-Modern exhibition space The Michael C. Carlos Museum is a combination art, ancient history, and archaeological museum with over 15,000 pieces in its permanent collection. It is housed in a 1916 Beaux Arts-designed building on the Emory University campus (Atlanta's most prestigious private college). Its contemporary interior, designed by the renowned architect Michael Graves, is a showcase in itself.

Ancient history The strength of this collection are early antiquities dating to 300 B.C. excavated from Middle Eastern countries, including artifacts from the ancient site of Babylon, Bronze and Iron Age pottery, oil lamps from Palestine, and a good collection of Egyptian mummies complete with their gold coffins and the treasures found inside. Throughout the museum, periods of history and the process of archaeology are re-created with artifacts and photographic displays, such as the replica of the excavation site at Jericho, filled with the remains of 25 human skeletons, and the excavation of Pharaoh burial sites in Egypt. There is also an excellent art and antique collection from early A.D. civilizations such as Rome, Central and South America, Mesopotamia, and Native American tribes. Its Pre-Columbian collection comprises 1,300 objects, including gold jewelry, pottery, and statues. It also has a sizable collection of drawings, prints, and illustrated manuscripts from the Middle Ages to the present, and a few French Impressionist paintings.

ATLANTA's *best*

MODERN ARCHITECTURE

A great architect

Atlanta owes a great portion of its modern Downtown skyline to home-grown architect John Portman who was educated at the Georgia Institute of Technology. His most famous structures are the Westin Peachtree Plaza Hotel, Atlanta Merchandise Mart, Gift Mart and Apparel Mart, Peachtree Center, Inforum, Hyatt Regency Atlanta Hotel, and One Peachtree Center. Although past retirement age, Portman continues to be active in his architectural firm.

The dramatic Downtown skyline

See Top 25 Sights for
HIGH MUSEUM OF ART (1983) ➤43

ATLANTA MARRIOTT MARQUIS (1985)
With tapered walls, the unusually designed 48-story-high atrium (that narrows as it gets higher), combined with the curvy balcony railing of each level, resembles the rib cage of a prehistoric animal. A gigantic fabric sculpture by French artist Daniel Graffin hangs within it.
✚ F6 ✉ 265 Peachtree Center Avenue ☎ 404/521-0000
🕐 24-hours hotel 🍴 5 restaurants, 4 bars 🚇 Peachtree Center (N1)

BUCKHEAD PLAZA BUILDING (1987)
At the heart of the Buckhead business district is this narrow 19-story neo-Gothic office tower with gabled top and flying buttresses extending downward from the third level. Alternating bands of green reflective glass and pink polished Canadian granite adorn its exterior walls.
✚ Off F1 ✉ 3116 Peachtree Road 🕐 Offices: business hours only; stores: 9–9 🍴 Good restaurants at lower level 🚇 23

FULTON COUNTY ADMINISTRATION COMPLEX (1989)
This airy and futuristic-looking building is a post-modern brick and glass structure composed of several units of differing heights connected to a central glass atrium. Its pseudo-ancient Grecian lobby with palm trees, sunken fountain, and columned archway offers a contrast to its otherwise modern surroundings.
✚ F7 ✉ 150 Pryor Street 🕐 Business hours only 🍴 Several restaurants, fast food outlets in nearby Underground Atlanta
🚇 Five Points (0)

GEORGIA-PACIFIC BUILDING (1982)
The rusty-red 52-story building, with its stair-stepping pyramid design at the upper levels, occupies hallowed ground on the site of Loew's Grand Theater (burned in 1978), where *Gone with the Wind* was premièred in 1939.
✚ F6 ✉ 133 Peachtree Street 🕐 Business hours only
🍴 Good restaurant ($$$)
🚇 Peachtree Center (N1)

NATIONSBANK PLAZA TOWER (1992)

This 53-story building, visible from many city locations, is the tallest in the South at 1,023ft. Its conical, multistory, open birdcage-like roof, topped by a large bronze spire, is its most prominent feature. A plaza and park surround it at ground level.

🏳 F5 ✉ 600 West Peachtree Street 🕑 Business hours only
🍴 Several restaurants in area 🚇 North Avenue (N3)

ONE ATLANTIC CENTER (1987)

The 50-story Gothic-inspired office tower, at 825ft tall, was Atlanta's tallest building from 1987 to 1992. Its copper pyramid roof, topped by a narrow steeple, is a city landmark visible from several locations.

🏳 F3 ✉ 1201 West Peachtree Street 🕑 Business hours only
🍴 Several restaurants in nearby Colony Square 🚇 Arts Center (N5)

ONE NINETY ONE PEACHTREE TOWER (1990)

Highly noticeable with its twin-towered neo-classical top, this 52-story office tower is a modern interpretation of the buildings found in America during the turn of the century, and offers a unique contrast to downtown Atlanta's more modern looking towers. A monumental arched entryway leads into an elaborate, six-story, skylit atrium lobby.

🏳 F6 ✉ 191 Peachtree Street 🕑 Business hours only
🍴 Several restaurants half a block north 🚇 Peachtree Center (N1)

ONE PEACHTREE CENTER TOWER (1992)

Downtown Atlanta's newest skyscraper features several slender, interconnecting towers of differing heights forming a jumbled, building-block pyramid top that is 60 stories high. Inside, a two-story lobby entered from four sides bridges a circular reflecting pool.

🏳 F6 ✉ 303 Peachtree Street 🕑 Business hours only
🍴 Excellent restaurant and café 🚇 Peachtree Center (N1)

RIO SHOPPING MALL (1989)

This unusual looking, two-story, U-shaped structure with garishly painted corrugated steel walls features the most bizarre plaza in the city. 350 large squatting bronze frogs ride on the surface of a reflecting pool lit by submerged fiberoptic strips and surrounding a white tubular sphere on the front lawn.

🏳 G5 ✉ 535 Piedmont Avenue 🕑 9–9 for stores, later for restaurants 🍴 3 restaurants in Mall 🚇 North Avenue (N3)

WESTIN PEACHTREE PLAZA HOTEL (1976)

The 73-story cylindrical tower sheathed in dark reflective glass, with its trademark external elevator and post-modern five-story atrium lobby, is the second tallest hotel in the world and primary focal point of the Atlanta skyline. The Sun Dial (► 69), a revolving bar and restaurant at its top, offers the best panoramic view of Atlanta.

🏳 F6 ✉ 210 Peachtree Street ☎ 404/659-1400 🕑 24-hour hotel 🍴 3 restaurants, 3 bars 🚇 Peachtree Center (N1)

Pencil Building

The narrow One Atlantic Center, by famed American architects John Burgee and Philip Johnson, with its pointed copper-covered roof and narrow steeple, is known as the "Pencil Building" by many residents. Others refer to it as the "IBM Building" due to its primary occupant. Despite several new buildings built around it in recent years, it is still the most prominent building in the Midtown area of Atlanta.

NationsBank Plaza Tower, Atlanta's tallest building

OLDEST BUILDINGS

A 20th-century city

When the Battle of Atlanta ended, very few buildings remained standing Downtown, most of it deliberately torched by Yankee troops. Because of this, Atlanta's architectural history belongs to the 20th century. The oldest buildings here are churches and those built from 1890 to 1930, a period of economic prosperity that resulted in the construction of the city's first skyscrapers.

The Flatiron Building

See Top 25 Sights for
STATE CAPITOL OF GEORGIA (1889) ➤27
JOEL HURT COTTAGE (1882) ➤34
TULLIE SMITH FARM (1845) ➤46

BULLOCH HALL (*c.* 1840)
This large Greek Revival *ante bellum* mansion features a pedimented portico supported by four massive Doric columns.
🚼 Off grid F1　✉ 180 Bulloch Avenue in Roswell
☎ 770/992-1731　🕐 Mon–Fri 10–2, guided tours　🍴 Several restaurants and fast food outlets along Roswell Road　🚇 Lenox (N7), then bus 85　💰 Inexpensive

CANDLER BUILDING (1906)
Built for Coca-Cola founder Asa G. Candler, the 17-story building has an elaborate decorated exterior with carved medallions of famous men, from Shakespeare to Einstein, and a marble staircase in its lobby.
🚼 F6　✉ 127 Peachtree Street　🕐 Business hours only
🍴 Several restaurants nearby　🚇 Peachtree Center (N1)

CAPITAL CITY CLUB (1911)
The five-story, Italian Renaissance-style house with projecting twin-columned porches is home to the city's oldest private club.
🚼 F6　✉ 7 Harris Street　🕐 Members only　🍴 Several restaurants, fast food outlets in nearby Peachtree Center Mall
🚇 Peachtree Center (N1)

DEKALB COUNTY HISTORIC COMPLEX (1822–40)
This complex features two *ante bellum*-style houses and the John Biffle Cabin (1822), a restored log and plank structure built by a Revolutionary War veteran, typical of the homes built by Atlanta's first settlers.
🚼 Off grid K6　✉ 720 West Trinity Place in Decatur
☎ 404/373-1088　🕐 Mon–Fri 9–4:30　🍴 Several restaurants, fast food outlets in downtown Decatur　🚇 Decatur (E6)　💰 Free

FLATIRON BUILDING (1897)
This 11-story triangular-shaped building, designed by influential architect Bradford Gilbert, was Atlanta's first skyscraper.
🚼 F6　✉ 84 Peachtree Street　🕐 Business hours only　🍴 Café
🚇 Five Points (0), Peachtree Center (N1)

GEORGIA RAILROAD FREIGHT DEPOT (1869)
This building, replacing the one torched by Union troops in the 1864 Battle of Atlanta, is now used as a meeting hall and for special events.
🚼 F7　✉ Depot Plaza; opposite The World of Coca-Cola　🕐 During special events only　🍴 Several restaurants, fast food outlets in nearby Underground Atlanta　🚇 Five Points (0)

HAMMONDS HOUSE (1857) ➤ 60

HEALEY BUILDING (1913)
One of Atlanta's most elegant early skyscrapers built in the neo-Gothic style with Tudor decorations and a rotunda lobby lit by natural light.
🞧 F6 ✉ 57 Forsyth Street 🕐 Business hours only 🚇 Five Points (0)

NATIONSBANK BUILDING (1901)
One of the first steel-framed structures built in America, the NationsBank Building features a sumptuous lobby and banking area with high ceilings, chandeliers, marble floors, and bronze desks.
🞧 F6 ✉ 35 Broad Street 🕐 Business hours only 🍴 Café 🚇 Five Points (0)

RHODES MEMORIAL HALL (1904)
Resembling a Rhine River castle with a four-story square tower and turreted roof, this house was built for a wealthy furniture chain-store owner. Its carved mahogany staircase, lined with nine stained-glass window panels depicting Civil War scenes is exquisite.
🞧 F2 ✉ 1516 Peachtree Street ☎ 404/881-9980 🕐 Mon–Fri 11–4 🍴 Several restaurants along Peachtree Street 🚇 Arts Center (N5) 🎫 Cheap

SHRINE OF THE IMMACULATE CONCEPTION (1873)
This Gothic-like church, complete with rose window and unequal towers, replaced the original building. This was spared by Sherman's troops after an impassioned plea by its pastor, Thomas O'Reilly, whose tomb is in the basement.
🞧 F7 ✉ 48 Martin Luther King, Jr. Drive 🕐 Daily 9–6; later when there are special events 🍴 Several restaurants, fast food outlets in nearby Underground Atlanta 🚇 Five Points (0)

STONE MOUNTAIN PARK PLANTATION (1790–1845)
Within Stone Mountain Park (➤38) are 19 plantation buildings brought from other Georgia locations, including an 18th-century house, 1845 *ante bellum* mansion, slave quarters, and barn (1800).
🞧 Off grid K4 ✉ East on US 78 (look for exit signs for Stone Mountain Park) ☎ 770/498-5600 🕐 Sep–May, daily 10–5.30; Jun–Aug, daily 10–9 🍴 Several restaurants ($$) and food concessions ($) throughout the park 🚇 Avondale (E7), then bus 120 🎫 Expensive (includes park entrance fee plus plantation entrance fee)

WIMBISH HOUSE (1898)
A French château look-alike with high-pitched mansard roof and turreted corner rooms, this is one of the few residential houses left on Peachtree Street. Now used as a dance club.
🞧 G3 ✉ 1150 Peachtree Street 🕐 Not open to public during the day 🍴 Several restaurants in nearby Colony Square 🚇 Midtown (N4), Arts Center (N5)

Progress?

Atlanta has suffered from two Sherman-like forces. The first was a Union general with a mission to destroy Atlanta. Fortunately, he had tunnel vision, as he skipped many buildings in the outlying areas. The other force is modern progress, whose developers value prime tracts of land over historical buildings. Due to the efforts of various historical preservation societies, buildings have been moved to protected sites.

A stained-glass window in Rhodes Memorial Hall

SMALL & UNIQUE MUSEUMS

Southeastern Railway Museum

Although it's off the beaten track, the Southeastern Railway Museum is a must see for train fanatics, with its collection of 40 steam and diesel locomotives, passenger and freight cars, and over 7,000 items of train memorabilia displayed in a former postal van. Its pride and joy is a miniature train built to scale, powered by a steam engine. It takes children for a 10-minute ride, complete with tunnel and bridge.

➕ Off grid G1 ✉ 3966 Buford Highway in Duluth ☎ 770/476-2013 🕐 Sat only 9–5 🚗 Requires a car to reach 🎟 Inexpensive

One of the many engines preserved in the Southeastern Railway Museum

APEX (AFRICAN-AMERICAN PANORAMIC EXPERIENCE) ►60

FEDERAL RESERVE MONETARY MUSEUM

This museum explains the history of money with exhibits of Native American trading beads, gem-stones, a 27-pound gold bar and $100,000 bills, and a complimentary packet of shredded bills to take home.
➕ F6 ✉ 104 Marietta Street ☎ 404/521-8747 🕐 Mon–Fri 9–4 🍴 Cafés along Marietta Street; Underground Atlanta five blocks away 🚇 Five Points (0) 🎟 Free

GEORGIA STATE MUSEUM OF SCIENCE AND INDUSTRY

This odd collection includes a mounted two-headed cow, squirrels playing poker, and other stuffed animals, plus displays of Georgia minerals, agriculture items, Native American artifacts, and military rifles.
➕ F7 ✉ 206 Washington Street in the State Capitol of Georgia (►27) ☎ 404/656-2000; recorded information 404/656-2844 🕐 Mon–Fri 8:30–5; Sat 10–4; Sun noon–4; closed all federal and state holidays 🍴 Cafeteria in building opposite 🚇 Georgia State (E1) 🎟 Free

HIGH MUSEUM OF ART FOLK ART AND PHOTOGRAPHY GALLERIES

This annex of the larger High Museum of Art (►43) exhibits American folk art and photography from its permanent collection and traveling shows.
➕ F6 ✉ 30 John Wesley Dobbs Avenue in Georgia-Pacific Building (►50) ☎ 404/577-6940 🕐 Mon–Sat 10–5 🍴 Good restaurants north on Peachtree Street 🚇 Peachtree Center (N1) 🎟 Free

MERCER MUSIC COLLECTION

Johnny Mercer, the songwriter who penned "Old Black Magic" and "Moon River," is honored here. Posters, record album covers, photographs, and his Grammy and Oscar awards are on display.
➕ F7 ✉ 103 Decatur Street in Pullen Library South, 8th floor ☎ 404/651-2477 🕐 Mon–Fri 8:30–5 🚇 Georgia State (E1) 🎟 Free

TELEPHONE MUSEUM

The history of Alexander Graham Bell's invention, from its earliest inception to current telestar and fiber optic technology, are explained through various exhibits and a 15-minute movie.
➕ F4 ✉ 675 West Peachtree Street, second floor (plaza level) in Southern Bell Center ☎ 404/223-3661 🕐 Mon–Fri 11–1 🍴 Cafeteria 🚇 North Avenue (N3; entrance into Southern Bell building) 🎟 Free

BATTLE OF ATLANTA SITES

See Top 25 Sights for
OAKLAND CEMETERY ►33

DEGRESS AVENUE BATTERY
On July 22, 1864, fierce fighting occurred when a Confederate brigade overran a Union artillery battery. They were repulsed later in the day after General Sherman spotted the attack from Copenhill (► 35). Historical markers guide you through the battle.
🔶 J6, K6 📧 Degress Avenue at DeKalb Avenue ⏰ 24-hours (avoid at night) 🍴 Several restaurants in nearby Little Five Points business district (►18) 🚇 Inman Park–Reynoldstown (E3)

ETERNAL FLAME OF THE CONFEDERACY
Opposite Underground Atlanta (► 29) is an old-fashioned gas street light that marks the site where a shell bounced off its post and exploded, fatally wounding a black barber.
🔶 F7 📧 Upper Alabama Street at Peachtree Street ⏰ 24-hours (avoid after midnight) 🍴 Several restaurants, fast food outlets in Underground Atlanta 🚇 Five Points (0)

FORT WALKER
South-east of Cyclorama (►25) are the remains of a Confederate artillery breastwork (with cannon) and defensive earthworks dug by slaves. It is named after General W. Walker who was killed near here.
🔶 H9 📧 Boulevard at Delmar Avenue in Grant Park ⏰ 24-hours (avoid at night) 🚌 31, 32 🎟 Free

KENNESAW MOUNTAIN NATIONAL BATTLEFIELD PARK ►20

MCPHERSON MONUMENT
An upturned cannon monument marks the spot where Union General James B. McPherson, one of Sherman's top commanders, was killed on July 22, 1864.
🔶 K8 📧 McPherson Avenue at Monument Avenue ⏰ 24-hours (avoid at night) 🚌 7

TANYARD CREEK PARK/COLLIER ROAD/PEACHTREE CREEK
It was in this area on July 20, 1864 that Confederate troops, detecting a gap in the Union line, staged a massive assault. After two hours of heavy fighting, they were driven back. Historical markers tell the story.
🔶 E1 📧 Collier Road halfway between Peachtree Road and Northside Drive ⏰ 24-hours (avoid at night) 🍴 Several restaurants along Peachtree Road 🚌 23

Killed in battle
During the night of July 21, 1864, weary Confederate troops withdrew from Peachtree Creek with orders to march toward Decatur where they could launch a surprise rear attack on the Union army. Instead, they encountered the fast advancing Union flank at dawn. By the end of the day on July 22, over 6,000 Confederate and 4,000 Union soldiers were dead.

This marker in Kennesaw Mountain National Battlefield Park outlines a key stage in the Battle of Atlanta, 1864

ATTRACTIONS FOR CHILDREN

See Top 25 Sights for
CENTER FOR PUPPETRY ARTS ➤45
FERNBANK MUSEUM OF NATURAL HISTORY ➤36
SCITREK ➤39
ZOO ATLANTA ➤24

Something for everyone

There are several places to take your children for education and entertainment in Atlanta that fit all budget ranges. If you choose the very expensive theme parks, be prepared to have fun too, since some of the rides and attractions are designed specifically for adults. To get your money's worth and to sample all the rides, plan on staying the entire day.

Six Flags Over Georgia

56

AMERICAN ADVENTURES/WHITE WATER ATLANTA

These two adjoining theme parks are a kid's dream come true. The former has an elaborate tree house costing over $1 million, 15 indoor and outdoor rides, miniature golf, race-car track, and Imagination Station that will keep your children busy for hours. The latter has 40 water attractions, including the largest kids' water playground in the country.

➕ Off grid D1   ✉ 250 North Cobb Parkway in Marietta ☎ 770/424-9283   🕐 Jun–Sep, Mon–Thu 11–7; Fri–Sun 10–9; hours vary rest of the year, so call in advance   🚗 Requires a car to reach   💰 Very expensive

CHATTAHOOCHEE NATURE CENTER

Animals, birds, and other creatures seen in their natural habitats are enjoyed by children of all ages. Nature trails and boardwalks wind through 100 acres of woodlands and wetlands bordering the Chattahoochee River.

➕ Off grid F1   ✉ 9135 Willeo Road   ☎ 770/992-2055   🕐 Daily 9–5   🚆 Lenox (N7), then bus 85   💰 Cheap

SIX FLAGS OVER GEORGIA

This is Atlanta's oldest theme park with more than 100 rides, many of them heart-stopping roller coasters (one goes in an upside down loop) and rides through water that you will want to save for last to avoid being damp all day. The park also features musical revues, high diving demonstrations, concerts by national artists, and other performances.

➕ Off grid A7   ✉ I-20W at 7561 Six Flags Road in Austell ☎ 770/739-3440   🕐 Jun–Sep, daily 10–10; Mar–May, mid-Sep–Oct Sat, Sun only; closed Nov–Feb   🍴 Several cafés, snacks areas   🚆 Hightower (W5), then Six Flags shuttle bus 201   💰 Very expensive

SOUTHEASTERN RAILWAY MUSEUM ➤54

YELLOW RIVER GAME RANCH

Spread over 24 acres are deer, rabbits, and an assortment of farm animals waiting to be fed and petted. Trails lead to a series of live animal viewing areas with buffalo, cougar, fox, skunk, porcupine, bobcat, and other wilderness creatures.

➕ Off grid K4   ✉ 4525 Highway 78 in Lilburn   ☎ 770/972-6643 🕐 Daily 9:30–6; Jun–Sep until 9   🚗 Requires a car to reach 💰 Moderate

FREE ATTRACTIONS

Atlanta has numerous free attractions. Yet some of the best will probably be those that you discover for yourself, such as self-guided tours of whatever interests you most, be it historical sights or antiques markets. Since space is limited for listing all the possibilities, categories for sights already described are noted, along with individual attractions not found elsewhere in this book.

THE CITY'S TOP 25 SIGHTS FOR FREE
Fernbank Science Center (► 37), Georgia Governor's Mansion (► 47), Inman Park (► 34), Martin Luther King, Jr. Tomb in the courtyard of the Center for Non-Violent Social Change (► 32), Michael C. Carlos Museum (► 48), Oakland Cemetery (► 33), State Capitol of Georgia (► 27), Underground Atlanta (► 29).

SMALL MUSEUMS FOR FREE (►54)
Federal Reserve Monetary Museum, Georgia State Museum of Science and Industry, High Museum of Art Folk Art and Photography Galleries, Mercer Music Collection, Southeastern Railway Museum, Telephone Museum.

OTHER CATEGORIES WITH FREE ATTRACTIONS
Modern Architecture (►50) Oldest Buildings (►52), Battle of Atlanta Sites (►55), Intown Neighborhoods (►58), Parks and Forests (►59).

ATLANTA CELEBRITY WALK
Atlanta's version of the Hollywood Walk of Fame includes the names of famous Georgians such as Ray Charles and Jimmy Carter etched into a marble walkway.
➕ F6 ✉ 235 International Boulevard (in front of Atlanta Chamber of Commerce building) 🕐 24-hours (avoid at night) 🍴 Restaurants in CNN Center opposite 🚇 Omni/Dome/GWCC (W1)

ATLANTA JOURNAL & CONSTITUTION GALLERY
An old type machine, front page news documenting historic events, and photographs of famous individuals who have worked for the city's daily newspaper.
➕ F6 ✉ 72 Marietta Street ☎ 404/526-5286 🕐 Mon–Fri 8–5 🚇 Five Points (0)

SWEET AUBURN CURB MARKET
Markets provide a good look at local traditions. This one specializes in southern "soul" foods such as collards, turnip greens, chitterlings, boiled peanuts, and every edible part of a pig but the oink. Come to observe and—if you dare—sample some food.
➕ J6 ✉ 209 Edgewood Avenue ☎ 404/659-1665 🕐 Mon–Sat 8–5:45 🍴 Café and deli food service; individual vendors 🚌 17, 99

The city of trees
Atlanta is still called the City of Trees, characterized by its beautiful neighborhoods lined with massive oak and dogwood trees sheltering the streets and homes. The word Peachtree is used in more than 32 street designations throughout metropolitan Atlanta and in several business names. It was derived through a misinterpretation of the Creek word for "pitch," the sap from pine trees that you are more apt to find here than the fruit tree, which grows better elsewhere in the South.

Intown Neighborhoods

See Top 25 Sights for INMAN PARK ➤ 34

The best addresses

To live in Buckhead means instant prestige. Therefore, as the city's most sought after address, it also has some of the most loosely defined boundaries which has spawned sub-Buckhead neighborhoods like SoBuck (south Buckhead), known for its abundance of art and antiques galleries and younger, trendier residents. The main route through Buckhead is on Peachtree Road, north of I-85.

ANSLEY PARK

This is one of Atlanta's most respected neighborhoods with large homes set back on hilly, landscaped lots. Developed 1904–1913, it quickly became a suburb for upper-class families.

➕ G2, G3 ✉ Just east of the High Museum of Art (➤ 43) bounded by 15th Street, Peachtree Street, Beverly Road and Piedmont Avenue 🍴 Several restaurants along Peachtree Street 🚇 Arts Center (N5)

BUCKHEAD

A large percentage of Atlanta's wealthy citizens live here. Over 105 million-dollar homes are found along the streets near the Governor's Mansion. Its main business district has the city's most interesting chic shops, restaurants and nightclubs found in one area.

➕ Off grid F1 ✉ Peachtree Road, East Paces and West Paces Ferry Roads, Roswell Road intersection (business district) 🕐 9–9 for stores, later for clubs, theaters, and restaurants 🍴 Numerous restaurants, cafés in Buckhead business district 🚌 23, 38, 40, 58

DRUID HILLS

Immaculate flower beds, shrubbery, and dogwood trees make this one of Atlanta's prettiest neighborhoods during the spring. It was developed in the early 1900s by Joel Hurt (of Inman Park fame) and famed landscape architect Frederick Law Olmsted.

➕ K4 and off grid at K4 ✉ Bounded by Briarcliff Road, Fairview Road, The By Way, Clifton Road 🚌 2, 6

MIDTOWN

The Midtown business district features a skyline comparable to Downtown, and the renovated mansions in its residential section make it a city showcase.

➕ F4, G4 ✉ Bounded by Ponce de Leon Avenue, Monroe Drive, Peachtree Street, 10th Street 🍴 Several restaurants along boundary streets 🚇 North Avenue (N3), Midtown (N4)

A Druid Hills mansion

VIRGINIA-HIGHLAND

Virginia-Highland, after a decade of young professionals buying and renovating homes in the area, is now the hot neighborhood to live in. The galleries, stores, bars, restaurants, and music clubs in its business district compete with Buckhead as the place to shop, dine, and party.

➕ J3 ✉ Virginia Avenue at North Highland Avenue (business district) 🕐 9–9 for stores, later for clubs, theaters and restaurants 🍴 Several restaurants 🚌 16, 45

PARKS & FORESTS

See Top 25 Sights for
STONE MOUNTAIN PARK ➤ 38

CHASTAIN MEMORIAL PARK
This park is best known for its outdoor amphitheater where nationally known musicians—classical, folk, rock, and jazz performers—play in summer concerts. It also has a golf course and other recreational facilities.
🞤 Off grid F1 ✉ 4469 Stella Drive ☎ 404/231-5888 (concert information), 404/733-5000 (tickets) 🕐 Varies depending on concert 🍴 Snack bars 🚌 38 🎫 Free for park; very expensive for concerts

CHATTAHOOCHEE NATURE CENTER
A large portion of the Chattahoochee River that slices through the north and west part of Atlanta, along with the land adjoining it, is protected by the federal government. It has 70 miles of trails ranging from flat and easy walks along the river to strenuous and steep climbs up river bluffs.
🞤 Off grid F1 ✉ 9135 Willeo Road, Roswell ☎ 770/992-2055 🕐 Daily 9–5 🚗 Requires a car to reach 🎫 Free

FERNBANK FOREST ➤ 37

OLYMPIC PARK
The 21-acre park is a beautiful landscaped area created from a decrepit warehouse district. It features a five-ring Olympic fountain, Olympic theme sculpture, and a surface paved with bricks engraved with the names of Olympic contributors.
🞤 F6 ✉ Between Atlanta Gift Mart and Inforum buildings via International Boulevard to CNN Center 🕐 24-hours (avoid at night) 🍴 Restaurants in Peachtree Center 🚇 Peachtree Center (N1)

PIEDMONT PARK
Closed to traffic, Atlanta's largest public park is very popular for jogging, bicycling, rollerblading, tennis, and other sports. Free concerts, festivals, and other events are held here throughout the year.
🞤 G3, H3 ✉ Piedmont Avenue between 10th and 14th Streets 🕐 24-hours (avoid at night) 🍴 Several restaurants nearby on 10th Street and Monroe Drive 🚌 31

STORZA WOODS (ATLANTA BOTANICAL GARDEN) ➤ 44

WOODRUFF PARK
The largest green space in Downtown Atlanta. On warm weekdays the park is filled with an interesting mix of office workers, street preachers, politicians, occasional protesters, students, and homeless people.
🞤 F6 ✉ Peachtree Street at Edgewood Avenue 🕐 24-hours (avoid at night) 🍴 Several restaurants, fast food eateries at nearby Underground Atlanta 🚇 Five Points (0)

Green spaces
Atlanta puts a high emphasis on green spaces. Throughout the city are parks of all sizes, providing oases of peace from the bustling city and room to play. Piedmont Park sets the standard. Its annual events draw people from afar and it provides enough open space to avoid feeling crowded.

Fishing in the Chattahoochee River

AFRICAN-AMERICAN ATTRACTIONS

See Top 25 Sights for SWEET AUBURN ▶32

The Herndon Home

ALONZO F. HERNDON HOME

This 15-room, Georgia Revival-style house (1910) exhibits the decorative furnishings, art collection and other family memorabilia of Atlanta's first black millionaire.

➕ D6 ✉ 587 University Place ☎ 404/581-9813 ⏰ Tue–Sat 10–4 🍽 Student cafeteria in Atlanta University complex 🚇 Vine City (W2) 🎫 Free

APEX (AFRICAN-AMERICAN PANORAMIC EXPERIENCE)

The history and culture of African-Americans in the United States is detailed here through permanent and temporary art and historical exhibits.

➕ G6 ✉ 135 Auburn Avenue ☎ 404/521-2739 ⏰ Tue–Sat 10–5 🚌 3, 74 🎫 Inexpensive

EBENEZER BAPTIST CHURCH

This church was the spiritual center for the 1960s Civil Rights movement and the site of Martin Luther King, Jr.'s funeral. Three generations of Kings preached from its pulpit.

➕ G6 ✉ 407 Auburn Avenue ☎ 404/688-7263 ⏰ Mon–Fri 9–4:30; Sat 11–2 🚌 3 🎫 Free

HAMMONDS HOUSE GALLERIES

The former mansion (1857) of the black anesthetist and arts patron, Otis T. Hammonds, is used as a gallery to display his African-American and Haitian art collection and as a resource center about African culture.

➕ C7 ✉ 503 Peeples Street ☎ 404/752-8730 ⏰ Tue–Fri 10–6; Sat, Sun 1–5 🚌 81 🎫 Inexpensive

MARTIN LUTHER KING, JR.'S BIRTHPLACE

Martin Luther King, Jr. was born in this modest Queen Anne-style house on January 15, 1929.

➕ H6 ✉ 501 Auburn Avenue ☎ 404/331-1590 or 404/331-3919 ⏰ Daily 10–5 🚌 3 🎫 Inexpensive

THE ROYAL PEACOCK

Still a popular music club, this was frequented in the late 1930s by jazz and blues greats such as Count Basie, Louis Armstrong, and Big Mabel, and in the 1960s by the king and queen of soul—James Brown and Aretha Franklin. Reggae and hip hop are played today.

➕ G6 ✉ 1861/2 Auburn Avenue ☎ 404/880-0745 ⏰ Daily 4PM–2AM 🍽 Drinks, snacks 🚌 3, 74 🎫 Cover charge

Atlanta's black heritage

Atlanta's history is directly tied to the role of black Americans, especially the 1960s Civil Rights movement leaders whose impassioned speeches were heard every week from Auburn Avenue church pulpits and meeting halls. Today, their efforts are being carried forward by black mayors and other politicians who have governed the city for the past two decades.

ATLANTA
where to...

SOUTHERN AMERICAN RESTAURANTS

Prices

Average meal per head, excluding drink

$ = up to $15

$$ = up to $35

$$$ = over $35

Southern style— from grits to iced tea

Southern foods are unique to this region. You won't find grits (coarsely ground corn cooked until creamy soft), barbecue (pit roasted chicken, pork or beef served with a tangy sauce), pot likker (liquid left from cooking vegetables), or collard greens (cabbage-like vegetable) on a menu anywhere else in America.

BURTON'S GRILL ($)

Exceptional fried chicken, hoe cakes, iced tea, and southern vegetables attract a regular clientele from blue-collar workers to executives. Get there early or you'll have to wait for a table.

🕂 J6 ✉ 1029 Edgewood Avenue opposite station ☎ 404/658-9452 🕔 6–4 🚇 Inman Park–Reynoldstown (E3) 🚌 17

THE COLONNADE ($)

Established in 1927, this Atlanta eating institution serves up some of the most authentic southern-style food anywhere. Cornish games hens, country fried steak, frog legs, and mouthwatering, made-from-scratch desserts keep this place constantly packed.

🕂 Off grid H1 ✉ 1879 Cheshire Bridge Road ☎ 404/ 874-5642 🕔 Mon–Sat 11–2:30, 5–9; Sun 11–8:30 🚇 No subway/train station nearby 🚌 27

KUDZU CAFE ($$)

Named after the broad-leafed vine that grows vigorously throughout the South, this restaurant offers nouveau southern cuisine and traditional favorites such as fried green tomatoes, grilled meat loaf, and moon pies. Good food, mountain lodge atmosphere, and a Buckhead address make this a popular dining establishment.

🕂 Off grid F1 ✉ 3215 Peachtree Road ☎ 404/262-0661 🕔 Sun–Thu 11–11; Fri, Sat until midnight 🚇 No subway/train station nearby 🚌 23

MARY MAC'S TEA ROOM ($)

This restaurant—serving specialties such as fried chicken, black eyed peas, sweet potato pie, cheese grits, and collard greens— is the place to see and to be seen, as all classes of people frequent it, from students to politicians.

🕂 G5 ✉ 224 Ponce de Leon Avenue ☎ 404/876-1800 🕔 Mon–Fri 11–8 🚇 North Avenue (N3) 🚌 2

PASCHAL'S ($)

Inexpensive southern "soul" food makes this a landmark restaurant. It was one of Martin Luther King, Jr.'s favorite places to dine. Today, you might sit next to a black musician or celebrity in town for a performance.

🕂 E7 ✉ 830 Martin Luther King, Jr. Drive ☎ 404/577-3150 🕔 5–midnight 🚇 Vine City (W2) 🚌 3, 53

SILVER GRILL ($)

This small diner serves up home-style southern cooking of the Old South. Excellent fried chicken, mashed potatoes and gravy, grilled pork chops, and vegetables.

🕂 H4 ✉ 900 Monroe Drive ☎ 404/876-8145 🕔 Mon–Fri, 10:30–9 🚌 27, 45

SILVER SKILLET ($)

Go here for breakfasts of ham, eggs, grits, red-eyed gravy, and home-made biscuits, or lunch specials of fried chicken, home-made corn bread, and traditional southern foods.

🕂 F3 ✉ 200 14th Street ☎ 404/874-1388 🕔 Mon–Fri 6–3; Sat 7–1; Sun 8–2 🚇 Arts Center (N5) 🚌 98

STANDARD AMERICAN RESTAURANTS

BACCHANALIA ($$$)

This California-style restaurant offers contemporary American cuisine with a hint of European flair that emphasizes fresh and healthy ingredients. Goat cheese–potato terrine, venison loin, mini rack of lamb with truffled mashed potatoes, and organically grown coffees are house specialties. It offers a fixed price menu, uncommon in American restaurants.

➕ Off grid H1 ✉ 3125 Piedmont Avenue ☎ 404/365-0410 🕐 Tue–Sat 6–10:30P.M. Ⓜ Buckhead (N7) 🚌 5, 38

BLUE RIBBON GRILL ($)

Owned by a local radio personality, who has decorated the walls with photographs of other celebrities, this cozy restaurant features delicious hand-cut steaks, chilli, home-made soups and desserts in a friendly setting.

➕ Off grid K1 ✉ 4006 LaVista Road ☎ 770/491-1570 🕐 Mon–Sat 11–2:30, 5:30–11 Ⓜ No subway/train station nearby 🚌 125

BONES ($$$)

Considered one of the top ten restaurants in Atlanta, it offers near perfect steaks in any form of cut or size you want, plus a great wine list in a club-like atmosphere. Haughty staff at times ignore newcomers, but you won't find a better steak in town.

➕ Off grid H1 ✉ 3130 Piedmont Road ☎ 404/237-2663 🕐 Mon–Fri 11:30–2:30; daily 6–11 Ⓜ Buckhead (N7) 🚌 5, 38

BUCKHEAD DINER ($$)

This glittering roadside diner straight out of the 1950s is frequented by a trendy and celebrity crowd. Good-quality American food including wild mushroom and veal meat loaf, lemon pie, B.L.T., and grilled pork chop with cheese grits.

➕ Off grid H1 ✉ 3073 Piedmont Road ☎ 404/262-3336 🕐 Mon–Sat 11–midnight; Sun 11–10 Ⓜ Buckhead (N7) 🚌 5, 38

MICK'S ($)

This popular and upbeat Atlanta chain has a variety of hamburgers, chicken dishes, salads, and cheesecake desserts to please everyone—all served up in a casual and friendly atmosphere.

➕ F7 ✉ 75 Upper Alabama Street at Underground Atlanta ☎ 404/525-2825 🕐 Daily 11A.M.–1A.M. Ⓜ Five Points (0) 🚌 3, 13, 17, 20, 42, 90, 97

THE VARSITY ($)

Atlanta's most famous eatery, straight out of the movie *American Graffiti*, has been serving up assembly-line hamburgers, chilli dogs, onion rings, chocolate malts, frosted orange, apple pie, and other typical drive-in fare since the early 1920s. Expanded several times, it still has awning-covered curb service for a few cars. Even if you are a health food addict, you need to eat here at least once; it's a one-of-a-kind experience.

➕ F5 ✉ 61 North Avenue ☎ 404/881-1706 🕐 Sun–Thu 7A.M.–12:30AM; Fri, Sat 7A.M.–2A.M. Ⓜ North Avenue (N3) 🚌 13, 66

Liquid refreshments

Just about anywhere, except for the more upscale restaurants, you'll find that Coca-Cola is king. The drink has been associated with Atlanta for so long that it would be a sacrilege to choose another cola. Remember, too, that if you order tea, it will automatically be sweet iced tea, unless you order otherwise.

FRENCH RESTAURANTS

French French

The best French restaurants in Atlanta tend to be run by chefs who are French natives or who were trained and worked in France. Part of the problem in achieving authenticity is lacking the proper ingredients completely to duplicate French recipes. These chefs are able to take American-grown foods and give them that special French touch.

ANIS ($$)

Three Frenchmen who met in Atlanta have created a bistro with excellent food based on traditional Mediterranean and Provençal recipes, especially the seafood, soups and lamb. Rotating the menu bi-monthly, they offer a hearty bouillabaisse seafood stew or a duck-lamb cassoulet.
⊞ Off grid F1 . ⊠ 2974 Grand-view Avenue ☎ 404/ 233-9889 ⏱ Tue–Sat 11:30– 2:30; Tue–Thu 6–10; Fri, Sat until 11; Sun 11:30–3, 6–10 ⓢ No subway/train station nearby 🚌 23, 40

BABETTE'S CAFÉ ($$)

Casual bistro-like restaurant with wood floors and brick walls serves up European country dishes with an emphasis on French favorites, including a fabulous cassoulet.
⊞ J5 ⊠ 471 North Highland Avenue ☎ 404/523-9121 ⏱ Tue–Sat 11:30–11; Sun 11:30–4 ⓢ No subway/train station nearby 🚌 16

BRASSERIE LE COZE ($$$)

This is the closest thing you'll find to a true Parisian brasserie in food and décor. Toulouse duck cassoulet, coq au vin, moules marinière, pot-au-feu, onion tarts, and fish dishes are delicious and well prepared. Delectable desserts and a good wine list.
⊞ Off grid K1 ⊠ Lenox Square Mall (► 70) ☎ 404/266-1440 ⏱ Mon–Thu 11:30–2:30, 5:30–10; Fri, Sat 11:30–11 ⓢ Lenox (NE7) 🚌 23, 25, 47, 48, 85, 92, 140

CASSIS ($$)

Named after a small Mediterranean village in France, it specializes in innovative seafood dishes from that area. Grilled, spiced shrimp with aubergine and roasted tomato coulis, and mixed grilled seafood with Mediterranean salsa, are two house specialties.
⊞ Off grid F1 ⊠ 3300 Peachtree Road in Hotel Nikko ☎ 404/365-8100 ⏱ Daily 7 A.M.–11 P.M. ⓢ Buckhead (N7) 🚌 5, 23, 38

CIBOULETTE ($$$)

Haute bistro fare such as Lyonnaise sausage and choucroute with lentils, field greens with Roquefort terrine, and liqueur-based desserts are served in an elegant atmosphere with an upper-class, dressy crowd. Open kitchen, mirrored walls, and close tables give it authenticity.
⊞ H2 ⊠ 1529 Piedmont Avenue ☎ 404/874-7600 ⏱ Mon–Thu 6–10; Fri, Sat 6–11 ⓢ No subway/train station nearby 🚌 31, 36

SOUTH OF FRANCE RESTAURANT ($$)

Owned by three brothers from Nice, this restaurant offers Mediterranean fare such as bouillabaisse and other seafood dishes, plus traditional lamb and veal dishes, and the classic onion soup gratinée. Its two fireplaces make it cozy on a winter evening.
⊞ Off grid H1 ⊠ 2345 Cheshire Bridge Road ☎ 404/325-6963 ⏱ Mon–Fri 11:30–2, 6–10:30; Sat until 11:30 ⓢ No subway/train station nearby 🚌 6, 27, 30, 33

ITALIAN RESTAURANTS

LA GROTTA ($$$)

Voted the best northern Italian restaurant for the last eight years, it could sit back on its laurels, but it doesn't. Try any veal or stuffed pasta dish and you'll leave satisfied. Even its most simplistic selections such as angel hair pasta with fresh garlic and basil are superb. Al fresco dining is available on a patio during summer.
🚇 Off grid F1 ✉ 2637 Peachtree Road ☎ 404/231-1368 🕐 Tue–Sat 6–10:30 🚇 No subway/rail station nearby 🚌 23

LUNA SI ($)

This trendy SoBuck neighborhood café features healthy, contemporary Italian cuisine. Menu changes monthly and features unique pasta dishes, fresh seafood, meat and vegetarian selections served in an artsy setting.
🚇 F2 ✉ 1931 Peachtree Street ☎ 404/355-5993 🕐 Tue–Sun 11–2:30, 5–11 🚇 Arts Center (N5) 🚌 23

PRICCI ($$)

This classy restaurant has a diverse northern Italian menu using recipes from the Tuscan, Ligurian, and Milanese regions, from home-made pastas to sea-food, meat and fowl dishes, plus luscious desserts.
🚇 Off grid F1 ✉ 500 Pharr Road ☎ 404/237-2941 🕐 Mon–Thu 11–11; Fri, Sat until midnight; Sun 5–10 🚇 No subway/rail station nearby 🚌 38, 40

ROCKY'S BRICK OVEN PIZZA ($)

Although called a pizzeria, it's more like a trattoria straight out of Italy, especially with its wood-burning oven imported from Milan, strings of cheese, sausage and garlic hanging from the ceiling, candle-lit tables covered with checked table cloths, classical music playing, and all types of Italian dishes on the menu. The chef here uses fresh ingredients and authentic Italian recipes.
🚇 F2 ✉ 1770 Peachtree Street ☎ 404/876-1111 🕐 Tue–Thu 11–10:30; Fri until midnight; Sat–Mon 4P.M.–midnight 🚇 Arts Center (N5) 🚌 23

SAN GENNARO ($$)

The menu here features classic southern Italian cuisine including fried calamari and hearty pasta dishes. Sausages and cheeses hanging from the ceiling remind you of an Italian trattoria. Very popular, so expect a long wait for a table.
🚇 Off grid H1 ✉ 2196 Cheshire Bridge Road ☎ 404/636-9447 🕐 Daily 5:30–11 🚇 No subway/train station nearby 🚌 27

VENI VIDI VICI ($$)

Expect the most superb Italian food here, especially spit roasted meats and fish dishes, antipasti selections, and huge portions of handmade pasta. The setting is elegant, with an open rotisserie and patio dining when warm outside.
🚇 F3 ✉ 41 14th Street ☎ 404/875-8424 🕐 Mon–Fri 11A.M.–midnight; Sat, Sun 5P.M.–midnight 🚇 Arts Center (N5) 🚌 23, 31, 36, 98

Restaurants for romance

La Grotta, with its luxurious interior, complete with checked tablecloths, candles, violinist, and hospitable staff, makes an ideal choice for a romantic evening. Next choice is San Gennaro for its authentic trattoria look.

OTHER INTERNATIONAL RESTAURANTS

Worldwide choice

Atlanta caters for a wide variety of palates, with gourmet food from all over the world. Make your choice from African, European, Asian, or American restaurants, with menus, both fun and formal, to tempt your palate and appropriate décor to match.

THE DINING ROOM ($$$)

This is the top rated restaurant in the city, a formal dining experience that will put a dent in your budget, but you won't leave disappointed. European food recipes include beet soup with crab cakes, sautéed *foie gras* with rhubarb, and goat cheese ravioli. The desserts will make you drool for more.
➕ Off grid F1 ✉ 3434 Peachtree Road in the Ritz-Carlton Buckhead Hotel ☎ 404/237-2700 🕐 Mon–Sat 6–10 🚇 Buckhead (N7), Lenox (NE7) 🚌 23, 25, 47, 48, 85, 92, 140

FLORENCIA RESTAURANT ($$$)

This elegant restaurant specializes in wild game and a blend of classic European dishes with American influences. Wild boar chops with baked gnocchi and seared elk chops are favorites, plus dishes such as rack of lamb and roasted yellow fin tuna are on the menu.
➕ F3 ✉ 75 14th Street in Occidental Grand Hotel ☎ 404/881-9898 🕐 Tue–Sat 6–11 🚇 Arts Center (N5) 🚌 23, 31, 36, 98

THE IMPERIAL FEZ ($$)

Resembling a Moroccan prince's tent, this fun restaurant allows you to recline on pillows at low tables and use your fingers to scoop up your meal of good couscous and stewed meats. Belly dancers add to the atmosphere.
➕ Off grid F1 ✉ 2285 Peachtree Road ☎ 404/351-0870 🕐 Daily 6–11 🚇 No subway/train station nearby 🚌 23

NIKOLAI'S ROOF ($$$)

This elegant roof-top restaurant (30th floor) with a dramatic view of the city specializes in Russian and classic French cuisine. Reservations are required since the five-course meal is only served twice each night.
➕ G6 ✉ 255 Courtland Street in Atlanta Hilton Hotel ☎ 404/659-2000 🕐 Daily 6:30P.M. and 9:30P.M. 🚇 Peachtree Center (N1) 🚌 16, 31, 46

REGGIE'S BRITISH PUB & RESTAURANT ($)

You won't want to miss this establishment. Its owner, a former royal marine, gives Atlanta its only truly authentic English pub. He offers a good mix of English and American favorites, including seafood chowder, bangers and mash, club sandwiches, and curried chicken.
➕ F6 ✉ 100 Techwood Drive in CNN Center ☎ 404/525-1437 🕐 Daily 11:30–11; open later when events are on at Omni Coliseum 🚇 Omni/Dome/GWCC (W1) 🚌 1, 11, 13, 18, 26, 50, 86

ROMANIAN RESTAURANT ($$)

This restaurant is the hot spot to dine for cuisine that features goulash, spicy sausages, stuffed cabbage, lamb, tortes, and home-made breads. The friendly staff will answer any of your questions about the menu.
➕ Off grid F1 ✉ 3081 East Shadowlawn Avenue ☎ 404/365-8220 🕐 Mon–Fri 11:30– 2:30; Mon–Sat 5:30–10:30 🚇 No subway/train station nearby 🚌 23, 40

SOUTHEAST ASIAN RESTAURANTS

CHA GIO ($)

For the past five consecutive years, this restaurant has been voted the number one Vietnamese establishment in Atlanta. Spicy chicken (they will make it milder upon request) and vegetarian dishes dominate the menu.

➕ G4 ✉ 966 Peachtree Street ☎ 404/885-9387 🕐 Daily 11–10 🚇 Midtown (N4) 🚌 10

FIRST CHINA ($)

This attractive restaurant with its personable staff is probably the best establishment among the large selection of Chinese restaurants in the Buford Highway corridor. Whole spiced fish, San-Shan soup, home-made noodles and sauce, and several meat and stir fry vegetable combinations are some of its offerings.

➕ Off grid K1 ✉ 5295 Buford Highway ☎ 770/457-6788 🕐 Daily 11:30 A.M.–3 A.M. 🚇 No subway/train station nearby 🚌 39

HONTO ($)

A favorite of Atlanta's Asian community, this restaurant offers a constantly changing seasonal menu based on authentic Hong Kong-style seafood dishes and other Chinese cuisine. Sampling its dim sum, the exotic rolling smorgasbord cart of appetizer-size dishes, is an experience.

➕ Off grid K1 ✉ 3295 Chamblee-Dunwoody Road in Chamblee ☎ 770/458-8088 🕐 Sun–Thu 11:30–10; Fri, Sat until 11 🚇 No subway/train station nearby 🚌 124

KAMOGAWA ($$$)

A very formal Japanese restaurant with four types of dining: sushi bar, regular table settings, teppanyaki grill tables, or the tatami room where you remove your shoes to sit on floor cushions. Excellent food served ceremoniously with traditional courses. Check out the green tea ice cream for dessert.

➕ Off grid F1 ✉ 3300 Peachtree Road in Hotel Nikko ☎ 404/841-0314 🕐 Daily 11:30–2, 6–10 🚇 Buckhead (N7) 🚌 23, 30, 38

LITTLE SZECHUAN ($)

If you like garlic-tinged Chinese dishes, this is the place. Favorites include near perfect garlic shrimp, eggplant with garlic, shredded pork with garlic sauce, and other recipes from central China.

➕ Off grid K1 ✉ 5091-c Buford Highway in Chamblee ☎ 770/451-0192 🕐 Wed–Mon 11–2, 5–11 🚇 No subway/train station nearby 🚌 39

SURIN OF THAILAND ($)

Scrumptious, spicy and authentic Thai food using fresh ingredients and sauces. One specialty is a crispy mee-krob, a pungent rice noodle dish with a tamarind sauce garnished with shrimp, eggs, and bean sprouts. Exotic drinks like mango daiquiris and the desserts are equally unique.

➕ J4 ✉ 810 North Highland Avenue ☎ 404/892-7789 🕐 Sun–Thu 11:30–10:30; Fri, Sat 11:30–11:30 🚇 No subway/train station nearby 🚌 16

Asian Atlanta

Want to visit the Far East without the high cost of getting there? Then head for Buford Highway in suburban Chamblee where you will find the city's Asian population. Lining this six-lane highway between Carol Avenue and I-285 (first exit west of I-85) are hundreds of Chinese, Japanese, Thai, Vietnamese, and Korean restaurants, markets, and businesses.

MEXICAN & LATIN RESTAURANTS

Mexican Atlanta

When the oil and construction business declined in Texas a decade ago, Mexicans moved to Atlanta in droves and the flood hasn't let up yet. To serve their own community, restaurants sprouted up everywhere. Several offer authentic Mexican dishes in re-created settings native to their homeland. Mexican food is usually good value for the dollar if you can stand the heat (highly spicy food).

CAFÉ TU TU TANGO ($)

Patterned after a Barcelona artist's loft, a visit here is a fun experience with strolling artists, musicians and others providing entertainment as you enjoy tasty Spanish tapas.
✚ Off grid F1 ✉ 220 Pharr Road ☎ 404/841-6222 🕐 Sun–Wed 11.30A.M.–midnight; Thu 11.30A.M.–1A.M.; Fr0i, Sat 11.30A.M.–2A.M. 🚇 No subway/ train station nearby 🚌 40

DON JUAN'S SPANISH RESTAURANT ($$)

The only place in Atlanta to get authentic Spanish (European) cuisine such as paella, chicken Espaniola and Zarzuela (seafood combination). Five courses are the norm, and there is live entertainment every night.
✚ Off H1 ✉ 1927 Piedmont Circle ☎ 404/874-4285 🕐 Mon–Sat 5–11 🚇 No subway/train station nearby 🚌 27, 31

EL CHARRO ($)

This lunch-only restaurant offers authentic Mexican cuisine with exceptional food and drink, including tacos, steak, tortillas, margaritas, and salsas.
✚ Off grid H1 ✉ 2581 Piedmont Road in Lindbergh Plaza Shopping Center ☎ 404/264-0613 🕐 11A.M.–2:30P.M. 🚇 Lindbergh (N6) 🚌 38, 39

EL TACO VELOZ ($)

Operated by a friendly Mexican family, it has great beef tacos, massive burritos, chile rellenos, and green salsa. Horchata, a sweetened rice drink, will help quench the fiery food.
✚ Off grid K1 ✉ 5084 Buford Highway ☎ 770/936-9094 🕐 Daily 10A.M.–9P.M. 🚇 No subway/train station nearby 🚌 39

LA PAZ ($)

For spicy Tex-Mex food and a rowdy atmosphere, this is the place. Hearty meat dishes excel, plus its salsas spooned on anything served to you will have you coming back for more. Good seafood if you prefer eating lighter.
✚ Off grid F1 ✉ 6410 Roswell Road ☎ 404/256-3555 🕐 Sun–Thu 5–10; Fri, Sat until 11 🚇 No subway/train station nearby 🚌 5

RIO BRAVA CANTINA ($)

When in Buckhead, this is the place for Mexican food and fun as a festival atmosphere prevails. Try the tortilla sandwiches, Carne Asade (a juicy skirt steak topped with green peppers, onions and Monterey Jack cheese), and Mexican sautéed shrimp.
✚ Off grid F1 ✉ 3172 Roswell Road ☎ 404/262-7431 🕐 Daily 11AM–midnight 🚇 No subway/ train station nearby 🚌 38

SUNDOWN CAFÉ ($)

Offers innovative Mexican and Latin dishes for reasonable prices. Sautéed shrimp cakes, Waco chilli, green chilli stew, and rancho mashed potatoes with jalepeno gravy are excellent, plus they have 15 versions of salsa dip.
✚ Off grid H1 ✉ 2165 Cheshire Bridge Road ☎ 404/231-1118 🕐 Mon–Fri 11–2; Mon–Thu 5:30–10; Fri, Sat until 11 🚇 No subway/train station nearby 🚌 27

ATLANTANS' FAVORITE RESTAURANTS

CITY GRILL ($$)

This posh downtown restaurant puts an innovative twist on traditional American and southern favorites with barbecue shrimp on grits, cumin-spiced salmon and chocolate-pecan soufflé pie. Very popular among business people, so expect to wait for a table during lunch hours.

✚ F7 ✉ 50 Hurt Plaza ☎ 404/524-2489 🕑 Mon–Fri 11:30–2:30, 5:30–10; Sat 11:30–2:30, 5:30–2:30A.M. 🚇 Five Points (0) 🚌 4, 17

DESSERT PLACE ($)

This is the Taj Mahal for Atlanta sweet tooths. Fat cream cheese brownies, pies, monstrous cakes, coffee concoctions, and much, much more. Yummy.

✚ J3 ✉ 1000 Virginia Avenue ☎ 404/892-8921 🕑 Sun–Thu 9A.M.–11:30P.M.; Fri 9A.M.–1A.M.; Sat 10A.M.–1A.M. 🚇 No subway/train station nearby 🚌 16, 45

57th FIGHTER GROUP RESTAURANT ($$)

Although the food is adequate, go here for the ambience. Located alongside the Peachtree-DeKalb Airport runway where you can watch the planes while you eat, it was built to resemble a World War II officers' club complete with sandbagged walls, piped in songs of the 1940s, and displays of photographs and other artifacts.

✚ Off grid K1 ✉ 3829 Clairmont Road ☎ 770/457-7757 🕑 Mon–Fri 11–2; Sun–Thu 5–10; Fri, Sat until 11 🚇 No subway/train station nearby 🚌 70

INDIGO COASTAL GRILL ($$)

Resembling a chic beach front café, sans the ocean view, this is one of the best places for seafood in town, whether it be New England lobsters, cod, and chowder, to lighter favorites reminiscent of the Caribbean. Shrimp dishes and Key lime pie are exceptional.

✚ K2 ✉ 1397 North Highland Avenue ☎ 404/876-0676 🕑 Daily 5:30–11 🚇 No subway/train station nearby 🚌 16

PANO AND PAULS ($$$)

The intimate and elegant setting of this restaurant, plus an often innovative menu, will make a return customer out of you. The food will capture and delight your palate—be it caviar with oysters, steak in herb sauce, or an eggplant terrine.

✚ Off grid F1 ✉ 1232 West Paces Ferry Road ☎ 404/261-3662 🕑 Mon–Fri 6–10; Sat 6–11 🚇 No subway/train station nearby 🚌 40, 58

SUN DIAL RESTAURANT & LOUNGE ($$)

Come here for the view, if not the food. On a clear day, from this revolving bar and restaurant sitting atop the 73-story-high hotel, are panoramic views of the entire city and far beyond. At night, it's awesome to see all the buildings lit up.

✚ F6 ✉ 210 Peachtree Street in Westin Peachtree Plaza Hotel ☎ 404/589-7506 🕑 Daily 11–2:30, 5:30–11 🚇 Peachtree Center (N1) 🚌 10, 13, 31

Spoilt for choice

Atlanta has one of the most vibrant restaurant scenes in America. With numerous transplants from other regions, plus a burgeoning foreign population, new restaurants sprout up every month that feature new and novel recipes. With so many restaurants to choose from, personal favorites are quickly replaced by something new.

ENCLOSED SHOPPING MALLS

Mall capital of America

No other city in the United States, except Chicago, can compete with Atlanta when it comes to mall shopping space. You'll see why indoor shopping is so popular if you arrive during the summer, when outside conditions can be torrid.

LENOX SQUARE MALL

The largest shopping mall in the Southeast with 268 shops. It has a broad mix with the Macy's, Rich's and Neiman Marcus department stores, several popular chain stores and specialty retailers such as Godiva Chocolatier; plus a food court, movie theater complex, and restaurants.
✚ Off grid H1 ✉ 3393 Peachtree Road at Lenox Road ☎ 404/233-6767; 800/344-5222 🕐 Mon–Sat 10–9:30; Sun 12:30–5:30 🚇 Buckhead (N7), Lenox (NE7) 🚌 23, 25, 47, 48, 85, 92, 140

THE MALL AT PEACHTREE CENTER

Beneath and at the rear of a fountained, open-air plaza surrounded by four corner-office towers are over 80 shops, restaurants, and services including a food court with a dozen fast food outlets.
✚ F6 ✉ 225 Peachtree Street ☎ 404/614-5000 🕐 Mon–Sat 10–6; Sun noon–5:30, but can vary 🚇 Peachtree Center (N1) 🚌 10, 13, 16, 31

NORTHLAKE MALL

In northeast Atlanta, has Macy's, J C Penney, Sears Roebuck, and the upscale Parisian department stores, food court and a couple of restaurants.
✚ Off grid K1 ✉ 4800 Briarcliff Road ☎ 404/938-5483 🕐 Mon–Sat 10–9:30; Sun 12:30–5:30 🚇 No subway/train station nearby 🚌 30, 91, 125

NORTH POINT MALL

With six department stores, this is the largest mall on the north side of metropolitan Atlanta. It has interesting specialty stores including Atlanta Brave's Clubhouse, Euro Art, Great Train, Smart Stuf, and Ozone Hi-Tech.
✚ Off grid G1 ✉ 1000 North Point Circle (off GA 400) in Alpharetta ☎ 770/740-9273 🕐 Mon–Sat 10–9:30; Sun noon–6 🚇 No subway/train station nearby 🚌 140 from Lenox (NE7) to Mansell Road "Park & Ride" lot, transfer to 141

PERIMETER MALL

This mall, located about 15 minutes north of Lenox Square Mall in the affluent suburb of Dunwoody, is known for quality family shopping with the High Museum of Art Gift Shop, Gap Kids, and The Nature Company. It also has Macy's and Rich's department stores.
✚ Off grid K1 ✉ 4400 Ashford-Dunwoody Road at I-285 ☎ 770/394-4270 🕐 Mon–Sat 10–9; Sun 12:30–5:30 🚇 Dunwoody (N9) 🚌 150

PHIPPS PLAZA

This three-level, 200-store mall caters to wealthy shoppers, with Saks Fifth Avenue, Bloomingdales, Lord & Taylor, Gucci, Parisian, Tiffany & Co, Abercrombie & Fitch, and several smaller specialty shops. It also has a movie theater complex, food court and a number of restaurants.
✚ Off grid K1 ✉ 3500 Peachtree Road at Lenox Road ☎ 404/261-7910 🕐 Mon–Sat 10–9; Sun noon–5:30 🚇 Buckhead (N7), Lenox (NE7) 🚌 23, 25, 47, 48, 85, 92, 140

DEPARTMENT STORES

J. C. PENNEY

This long established chain caters to the needs of the middle class. Affordable clothes and very strong furniture departments.

⊞ Off K1 ✉ Northlake Mall, 4800 Briarcliff Road, and five other malls ☎ 404/434-2561, 800/222-6161 🕒 Mon–Sat 10–9:30; Sun 12:30–6 🚇 No subway/train station nearby 🚌 30, 91, 125

MACY'S

The downtown location of this department store – housed in a six-story, Italian villa-style building – first opened for business as Davisons (department store) in 1927. Offering a broad range of goods, with especially good clothing, gourmet foods and kitchen accessory departments, it is the last of the grand department stores (chandeliers, marble floors and high ceilings) left in Atlanta that isn't connected to a mall.

⊞ F6 ✉ 180 Peachtree Street and eight malls ☎ 404/221-7221, 800/456-2297 🕒 Mon–Sat 10–6; Sun noon–6 🚇 Peachtree Center (N1) 🚌 10, 13, 16, 31

NEIMAN MARCUS

This famed department store catering to the needs of the upper class has been a mainstay of Lenox Square Mall for over two decades. Even if you don't have the money, the merchandise, especially during the Christmas season, is fun to look at. Precious jewelry, perfume and designer-label clothing departments are its trademark.

⊞ Off grid K1 ✉ Lenox Square Mall 3393 Peachtree Road at Lenox Road ☎ 404/266-8200 🕒 Mon–Sat 10–9:30; Sun 12:30–5:30 🚇 Buckhead (N7), Lenox (NE7) 🚌 23, 25, 47, 48, 85, 92, 140

PARISIAN

This chain store offers classic and semi-upmarket goods to a wide clientele. Most helpful staff of any chain store in Atlanta. Recent entry into the Atlanta market brings a bit of class to its mall scene.

⊞ Off grid K1 ✉ Phipps Plaza, 3500 Peachtree Road at Lenox Road and three other malls ☎ 404/814-3200 🕒 Mon–Sat 10–9; Sun noon–5:30 🚇 Buckhead (N7), Lenox (NE7) 🚌 23, 25, 47, 48, 85, 92, 140

RICH'S

Rich's is considered the city's best department store chain with well planned shops and a variety of goods at prices slightly lower than Macy's.

⊞ Off grid K1 ✉ Lenox Square Mall 3393 Peachtree Road at Lenox Road and 11 other malls ☎ 800/282-8800 🕒 Mon–Sat 10–9:30; Sun 12:30–6 🚇 Buckhead (N7), Lenox (NE7) 🚌 23, 25, 47, 48, 85, 92, 140

SAKS FIFTH AVENUE

A branch of the famous high fashion department store brings New York sophistication to Atlanta. Buy designer clothes, shoes, furs and perfumes.

⊞ Off grid K1 ✉ Phipps Plaza 3500 Peachtree Road at Lenox Road ☎ 404/261-7234 🕒 Mon–Fri 10–9; Sat 10–7; Sun 12:30–5:30 🚇 Buckhead (N7), Lenox (NE7) 🚌 23, 25, 47, 48, 85, 92, 140

Shopping paradise

If you ask visitors from other southern locations why they come to Atlanta, the answer will probably be: 1) to visit relatives; 2) to attend a convention; 3) sports; 4) entertainment; or 5) shopping (number 1 among females). Between Miami and Washington, DC, Atlanta is a mecca for shoppers. If you can't find it here, it won't be anywhere else.

ANTIQUES SHOPS & DISTRICTS

Antiques galore

You can "shop until you drop" and still not hit all the antiques shops in Atlanta. Although the greatest concentration of them is in the sprawling Buckhead neighborhood and suburban Chamblee, consider renting a car to venture to the outer suburbs of Roswell, Norcross and Buford where you will find several outstanding shops.

ATLANTA FLEA MARKET AND ANTIQUE CENTER

In this 80,000 square foot warehouse setting are 150 dealers selling antique furniture and decorative items (primarily American and English), collectibles, glassware and other items. ⊞ Off grid K1 ⊠ 5360 Peachtree Industrial Boulevard in Chamblee ☎ 770/458-0456 ⏱ Fri, Sat 11–7; Sun noon–7 🚇 Chamblee (N9) 🚌 25

BENNETT STREET GALLERIES

This former street of warehouses now contains over 150 art galleries, and antiques shops. The Stalls (116 Bennett Street) features 75 antiques and decorative art furnishings dealers and another 45 dealers are in the Interiors Market (55 Bennett Street). It's a fun place for buying and browsing. ⊞ Off grid F1 ⊠ Bennett Street off Peachtree Road (2100 block) ⏱ Daily 9–6 (some shops have later hours) 🚇 No subway/train station nearby 🚌 23

CHAMBLEE'S ANTIQUE ROW

In historic 19th-century homes, shops and former churches along Broad Street and Peachtree Road in suburban Chamblee are over 200 antiques and collectibles dealers. Whatever you are looking for, especially 19th- and early 20th-century furniture and knickknacks, will probably be found here. ⊞ Off grid K1 ⊠ Broad Street at Peachtree Road ⏱ Mon–Sat 10:30–5; Sun 1–5, for most shops 🚇 Chamblee (NE9) 🚌 129, 132

MIAMI CIRCLE

On the fringe of Buckhead is a street lined with over 34 quality antiques and decorative arts dealers. Le Primitif Gallery (631 Miami Circle) specializing in antiques from Haiti is interesting, and Williams Antiques (631-B Miami Circle) is Georgia's oldest antiques business. ⊞ Off grid H1 ⊠ Miami Circle, off Piedmont Road about two miles from I-85 ⏱ Most are open Mon–Sat 10–6; Sun noon–5 🚇 Lindbergh (N6) 🚌 38, 39

20TH CENTURY ANTIQUES

This shop in the popular Virginia-Highland business district has an eclectic combination of antique objects, including old furniture, radios, southwestern accent pieces, silver mirrors, art deco items, and Limoges plates. ⊞ J3 ⊠ 1044 North Highland Avenue ☎ 404/892-2065 ⏱ Mon–Wed 1–7; Thu–Sat 11–9; Sun noon–6 🚇 No subway/train station nearby 🚌 16, 45

THE WRECKING BAR

Housed in a National Register, 19th-century home near the Little Five Points business district, this antiques shop has 18,000 square feet of architectural antiques including doors, mantels, light fixtures, stained glass windows, porch pedestals, and hardware. ⊞ K6 ⊠ 292 Moreland Avenue ☎ 404/525-0468 ⏱ Mon–Sat 9–5 🚇 Inman Park-Reynoldstown (E3) 🚌 3, 48

Art & Southern Handicrafts Galleries

ALIYA–THE GALLERY OF MORNINGSIDE

This gallery represents 30 of the region's hottest artists in painting, sculpture, glass, and mixed media. Exceptional work by the next generation of great artists; buy it while it is still affordable.
✚ K2 ✉ 1402 North Highland Avenue, Suite 4
☎ 404/892-2835 🕐 Tue–Sun 11–10 Ⓢ No subway/train station nearby 🚌 16

BERMAN GALLERY

Specializing in ceramics, paintings and other creations by southern crafts people such as Minnie Evans, this was the first gallery in Atlanta to show the religious-oriented folk paintings of Howard Finster, a former Georgia preacher and now an internationally recognized artist. He has done album covers for the rock bands Adam Again, REM, and Talking Heads.
✚ Off grid F1 ✉ 3261 Roswell Road ☎ 404/261-3858
🕐 Tue–Sat 10–5 Ⓢ No subway/train station nearby 🚌 38

FAY GOLD GALLERY

Fay Gold is noted for her cutting-edge shows of nationally and internationally renowned contemporary artists, photographers and sculptors. The works exhibited here are usually modern and often controversial, such as the photographs of Robert Mapplethorpe.
✚ Off grid F1 ✉ 247 Buckhead Avenue
☎ 404/233-3843
🕐 Mon–Sat 9:30–5:30 Ⓢ No subway/train station nearby 🚌 23, 38, 40

FORM AND FUNCTION GALLERY

Instead of art that you hang on your wall, this gallery specializes in functional pieces with an artsy bent. Chairs, tables, lamps, bowls and other familiar objects appear in creative and whimsical forms. A recent set of chairs on display were created from car gas tanks.
✚ J4 ✉ 784 North Highland Avenue, Suite 5
☎ 404/892-3193 🕐 Thu–Sat noon–10; Tue and Sun noon–6, Wed until 7 Ⓢ No subway/train station nearby 🚌 16

JACKSON FINE ART GALLERY

This is the best place to buy photography by world renowned 20th-century American and European photographers such as Ansel Adams, Walker Evans, Bill Brandt, Henri Cartier-Bresson, Robert Doisneau, Edward Weston, and others.
✚ Off grid F1 ✉ 3115 East Shadowlawn Avenue
☎ 404/233-3739 🕐 Mon–Fri 9–6; Sat 10:30–5:30 Ⓢ No subway/train station nearby
🚌 23, 40

SIGNATURE SHOP AND GALLERY

This is the oldest crafts-only gallery in the country with handmade artistic and functional works from fiber, clay, metal, wood, glass, and paper by regional and nationally recognized crafts people.
✚ Off grid F1 ✉ 3267 Roswell Road ☎ 404/237-4426
🕐 Mon–Sat 10–5 Ⓢ No subway/train station nearby
🚌 38

Naturally crafty

The Southern Appalachian region that Atlanta belongs to geographically has a long history of crafts people producing artistic and functional pieces out of available natural products. With an abundance of clay and forests, Georgia has some of the nation's best potters and woodworkers. When you are gallery hopping, make sure you include some of the galleries that specialize in crafts.

BOOKSTORES

Books galore

There is no shortage of bookstores in Atlanta as every national chain has at least one shop here. For discounted bestsellers and standard titles, the B. Dalton Booksellers and Waldenbooks found at every mall are adequate. A step above them are Barnes & Noble Bookstore and Borders Book Shop, two national chains that offer a better selection. For more specialized titles, check out the city's independent bookshops.

THE ARCHITECTURAL BOOKSTORE

This small bookshop, run by the American Institute of Architects (AIA), has books about Atlanta architecture, and other world locations, travel guides and a few art books. It also has an interesting selection of greeting cards, T-shirts, and unusual gifts.
F6 ✉ The Mall at Peachtree Center (► 70)
☎ 404/222-9920 🕐 Mon–Sat 10–6 🚇 Peachtree Center (N1)
🚌 10, 13, 31

THE BOOK NOOK

This is the largest second-hand bookshop in Atlanta with over 200,000 titles priced at 60 percent of the original retail price. It also sells second-hand music cassette tapes, CDs, record albums, comic books, current magazines, and some current books.
Off grid K1 ✉ 3342 Clairmont Road
☎ 404/633-1328 🕐 Daily 10–11 🚇 No subway/train station nearby 🚌 19, 39, 70

BORDERS BOOK SHOP

Borders' large new shop boasts 120,000 book titles, 60,000 CDs and cassettes, 8,000 videos, and a café. Although it is a chain establishment, it stocks a variety of abstruse titles.
Off grid K1 ✉ Peachtree Road at East Roxboro Road
☎ 404/237-0707
🕐 Mon–Sat 9–9; Sun 11–6
🚇 No subway/ train station nearby 🚌 25, 85, 92, 140

CHARIS BOOKS

This long established Little Five Points bookshop specializes in feminist books, cassettes, cards, T-shirts, and more. Special programs every Thursday night at 7:30P.M.
K5 ✉ 1189 Euclid Avenue
☎ 404/524-0304 🕐 Mon, Tue, Thu 10:30–6:30; Wed 10:30–8; Fri, Sat 10:30–10; Sun noon–6 🚇 Inman Park–Reynoldstown (E3) 🚌 3, 48

OXFORD BOOKS

Oxford is the largest independent bookstore in the southeast United States. Its main store, featuring weekly book signings by famous authors, also has a large magazine and newspaper section (including some from Europe), rare books and collectibles section, video department, and sells sheet music, tapes and CDs. On its upper level, the Arts Connection gallery exhibits local artists' work and the Espresso Café serves light meals, coffee, beverages, and desserts.
Off grid F1 ✉ 360 Pharr Road; two other locations
☎ 404/262-3333
🕐 Sun–Thu 9A.M.–midnight; Fri, Sat 9A.M.–2A.M. 🚇 No subway/train station nearby
🚌 23, 38, 40

TALL TALES

This small shop, run by a very knowledgable staff, excels in regional fiction and travel books. Expanded recently, it now includes a small coffee/dessert shop.
Off grid K1 ✉ 2999 North Druid Hills Road in Toco Hills Shopping Center
☎ 404/636-2498 🕐 Mon–Sat 10:30–9; Sun 12:30–6:30
🚇 No subway/train station nearby 🚌 8, 30

CLOTHING: MEN

BENNIE'S DISCOUNT SHOES

When Atlanta men need fine dress or casual shoes, they head for Bennie's. All major brand names are discounted, some as much as 75 percent on their bargain tables.

Off grid H1 ⊠ 2581 Piedmont Road in Lindbergh Plaza Shopping Center ☎ 404/262-1966 ⏰ Mon–Sat 8–6 🚇 Lindbergh (N6) 🚌 38, 39

BROOKS BROTHERS

America's oldest clothing company, established in 1818, has high quality men's wear in traditional cuts and fabrics. Good selection of suits, shirts, and ties.

F6 ⊠ The Mall at Peachtree Center and Lenox Square Mall (▶ 70) ☎ 404/577-4040 ⏰ Mon–Sat 10–6 🚇 Peachtree Center (N1), Lenox (NE7) 🚌 10, 13, 31

FRIEDMAN'S SHOES

This shop became popular when professional athletes began telling their fellow athletes and friends about it. With sizes ranging from 7 to 20 (width A–EEE), visiting team buses can often be seen at the entrance. Autographed balls, shirts, and photographs are displayed.

F7 ⊠ 209 Mitchell Street; two other locations ☎ 404/524-1311 ⏰ Mon–Sat 9–5:30 🚇 Five Points (0) 🚌 1

INTERNATIONAL MAN

Upscale boutique features sophisticated and fashionable clothes with an emphasis on Italian designers such as Canali, Pancaldi, Moschino, and Gianfranco Ferre.

Off grid K1 ⊠ Phipps Plaza (▶ 70) ☎ 404/841-0770 ⏰ Mon–Sat 10–9; Sun noon–5:30 🚇 Buckhead (N7), Lenox (NE7) 🚌 23, 25, 47, 48, 85, 92, 140

MEN'S WEARHOUSE WAREHOUSE

This is one of three nation-wide clearance shops for this national men's clothing chain. Thousands of designer suits, shirts, ties, and accessories are discounted. Suits can be bought for less than $200, shirts and ties for less than $15.

C1 ⊠ 1218 Old Chattahoochee Avenue ☎ 404/351-1060 ⏰ Mon–Sat 10–7; Sun noon–6 🚇 No subway/train station nearby 🚌 1

MUSES

This home-grown company has been attiring men in classic styles since 1879, with good suits in the $400–$600 range. Pick out the perfect suit with expert help from a friendly staff. On-site tailoring and alterations.

F6 ⊠ The Mall at Peachtree Center (▶ 70); four other locations ☎ 404/420-4520 ⏰ Mon–Fri 9:30–6; Sat 10–6 🚇 Peachtree Center (N1) 🚌 10, 13, 31

SEBASTIAN'S CLOSET

The top men's clothing fashions are sold here, including clothes by the designers Hugo Boss, Pal Zileri, Vestimenta, Zanella, Jhane Barnes, and Donna Karan.

Off grid F1 ⊠ 3222 Peachtree Road ☎ 404/365-9033 ⏰ Mon–Sat 10–6; Thu until 8 🚇 No subway/train station nearby 🚌 23

Department store choice

Unless you are looking for a particular look, the men's departments at Macy's, Parisian, and Rich's offer a good selection of quality ready-to-wear clothes. For easy selection, all of them are compartmentalized, with ties in one section, shirts, suits, etc. They also have specific areas devoted to individual designers such as Americans Ralph Lauren and Alexander Julian.

CLOTHING: WOMEN

Vintage and retro to go

Vintage and retro clothes are part of the "in" look in the 1990s. The best stores to find these type of clothes are in Little Five Points, most notably Stefan's Vintage Clothing (1160 Euclid Avenue), The Junkman's Daughter (1130 Euclid Avenue), and Pink Flamingos (1166 Euclid Avenue). Other good places include consignment shops and thrift shops that are spread throughout the city.

AJS SHOE WAREHOUSE

For women's shoes, this is the best, with major brand names available at great discounts.

➕ C3 ✉ 1788 Ellsworth Industrial Boulevard ☎ 404/355-1760 ◷ Fri, Sat 10–6 🚇 No subway/train station nearby 🚌 1

BACKSTREET BOUTIQUE

Buckhead's quality resale consignment shop where you can look like a million dollars for a fraction of the price. Adolfo, Chanel, and Donna Karan are among the brands you find here.

➕ Off grid F1 ✉ 3655 Roswell Road ☎ 404/262-7783 ◷ Tue–Fri 11–6; Sat 10–5 🚇 No subway/train station nearby 🚌 23, 38

MITZI & ROMANO

This shop sells cutting-edge American and European clothes, jewelry, and accessories from designers such as Kenar, French Connection, and Betsey Johnson.

➕ J3 ✉ 1038 North Highland Avenue ☎ 404/876-7228 ◷ Mon 11–8; Tue–Thu until 9; Fri, Sat until 10; Sun noon–7 🚇 No subway/train station nearby 🚌 16, 45

RENÉ RENÉ

These shops are a showcase for the creations of local fashion designer René Sanning, known for her avant-garde and original designs with a combination modern/1940s retro-look, including interesting accessories.

➕ F2, K5 ✉ 1776 Peachtree Street, 1142 Euclid Avenue in Little Five Points (▶ 18)

☎ 404/875-7883, 404/522-RENE ◷ Mon–Fri 11:30–6:30; Sat 11–7; Sun 1–5 🚇 Arts Center (N1), Inman Park–Reynoldstown (E3) 🚌 23, 16, 48

REXER-PARKES

This classy shop sells fashionable clothes for women who wear junior sizes. When you need a little black dress or a complete wardrobe for the office, this is the place. Good selection of weekend casual wear, lingerie, and accessories too.

➕ Off grid F1 ✉ 2140 Peachtree Road in Brookwood Square Shopping Center ☎ 404/351-3080 ◷ Mon–Wed, Fri 10–7; Thu 10–9; Sat 10–6 🚇 No subway/train station nearby 🚌 23

SASHA FRISSON

This is the place to find the latest haute couture fashions by Moschino, Karl Lagerfeld, Thierry Mugler, and Givenchy. Specializes in separates, classic sportswear, leather apparel, and fabulous evening wear, plus all the accessories.

➕ Off grid F1 ✉ 3094 East Shadowlawn Avenue ☎ 404/231-0393 ◷ Mon–Sat 10–6 🚇 No subway/train station nearby 🚌 23, 40

STONE MOUNTAIN HANDBAG FACTORY STORE

This company is known throughout the South for its high quality leather handbags and purses at 20–50 percent off the retail price.

➕ Off grid K4 ✉ 963 Main Street in Stone Mountain ☎ 770/498-1316 ◷ Mon–Sat 10–6; Sun 1–5 🚇 No subway/train station nearby 🚌 118, 120

FINE GIFTS & SOUVENIRS

ARTLITE
Although primarily an office supply shop, it has the best selection of pens in Atlanta, including major brands such as Mont Blanc, Parker, Colibri, Visconti, Waterman, Cross, Lamy, and Sheaffer.
🗺 H1 ✉ 1851 Piedmont Road ☎ 404/875-7271 🕐 Mon–Fri 8–6; Sat 9–5 🚇 No subway/train station nearby 🚌 31

CITY ART WORKS
This shop sells uniquely designed crafts that emphasize function as well as design. There's furniture, dinnerware, tabletop items for the home and office, jewelry, mirrors, picture frames, candle holders, and decorative objects.
🗺 Off grid F1 ✉ 2140 Peachtree Road in Brookwood Square Shopping Center ☎ 404/605-0786 🕐 Mon–Wed, Sat 10–6:30; Thu, Fri until 8 🚇 No subway/train station nearby 🚌 23

GIFTS EXTRAORDINAIRE
Looking more like an art gallery, this small gift shop sells a wide array of interestingly designed decorative objects, including metal crafted creations and wall sculpture, mobiles, raku pottery, and candles.
🗺 Off grid K1 ✉ Phipps Plaza (➤ 70) ☎ 404/365-9231 🕐 Mon–Sat 10–9; Sun noon–5:30 🚇 Buckhead (N7), Lenox (NE7) 🚌 23, 25, 47, 48, 85, 92, 140

MUSEUM SHOP
This store has fine art books, jewelry, prints, games, clothes, and other items all under one roof from the gift shops of some of America's best museums.
🗺 Off grid K1 ✉ Phipps Plaza (➤ 70) ☎ 404/365-8019 🕐 Mon–Sat 10–9:30; Sun 12:30–5:30 🚇 Buckhead (N7), Lenox (NE7) 🚌 23, 25, 47, 48, 85, 92, 140

THE SHARPER IMAGE
This San Francisco chain offers an eclectic group of gift-oriented items ranging from clothes, shoes and jewelry to sophisticated electronic calculators and language converters, as well as health-oriented products such as massagers and exercise equipment, and a variety of sophisticated toys. The 60-day trial period for any item you may buy is a bonus.
🗺 Off grid K1 ✉ Lenox Square Mall (➤ 70) ☎ 404/261-8388 🕐 Mon–Sat 10–9:30; Sun 12:30–5:30 🚇 Buckhead (N7), Lenox (NE7) 🚌 23, 25, 47, 48, 85, 92, 140

A TOUCH OF GEORGIA
This is the perfect place for a gift item to remind you of your stay here. There are numerous Georgia theme items such as T-shirts and coffee mugs with a peach (a state emblem) or state map printed on them, plus numerous edible products such as Muscadine jelly and peach butter created from foods grown in Georgia.
🗺 F6 ✉ The Mall at Peachtree Center (➤ 70) ☎ 404/577-6681 🕐 Mon–Sat 10–6 🚇 Peachtree Center (N1) 🚌 10, 13, 31

Sports gifts
What constitutes a great gift all depends on who you are buying it for. If you are not sure of the person's interests, buy them something that says Atlanta. Being a professional sports town, there are several stores like the Brave's Clubhouse (CNN Center) to buy authentic shirts, uniforms, caps, T-shirts, and other novelty items representing the teams. If you get to an actual game, game programs are a good item to buy.

HALLS & ARENAS

Buying tickets

The cost of living in the South as a whole is often cheaper than the rest of the nation, but don't expect Atlanta entertainment to fit into this category. National acts cost no less here than anywhere else. Most entertainment spots sell tickets directly through their own box offices or they can be obtained from TicketMaster (☎ 404/249-6400 or 800/326-4000). Consult the *Atlanta Journal & Constitution's* Friday "Weekend Preview" or Saturday "Leisure" tabloid sections about forthcoming events (► 93).

ATLANTA CIVIC CENTER

With its large stage, this is a favorite venue of theater companies and other groups who need a lot of space. With no obstructing pillars, this concert hall has good sight lines.
➕ G5 ✉ 395 Piedmont Avenue ☎ 404/523-6275 🚇 Civic Center (N2) 🚌 16, 46

CHASTAIN PARK AMPHITHEATER

Many Atlantans look forward to Chastain's summer concert series that offers music from the Atlanta Symphony Orchestra to blues rocker Bonnie Raitt, country star Willie Nelson, and New Age musician Yanni. Several levels of seating are available, from sitting at a table where you can dine to a space on the lawn (bring a blanket from your hotel).
➕ Off grid F1 ✉ 4469 Stella Drive ☎ 404/733-5000 (tickets), 404/231-5888 (concert information) 🚇 No subway/train station nearby 🚌 38

COCA-COLA LAKEWOOD AMPHITHEATER

From May to the end of October, rock music concerts are held at this outdoor amphitheater that accommodates 18,000 people. The Allman Brothers, Rod Stewart, Eric Clapton, and other popular acts have performed here.
➕ E13, F13 ✉ 2002 Lakewood Way ☎ 404/627-9704 🚇 No subway/train station nearby 🚌 Shuttle bus from Lakewood–Fort McPherson station (S4), or 17, 100

FOX THEATRE

For many Atlantans, this is the number one place to view entertainment (► 41). With only 4,518 seats it is intimate and the acoustics are good. A regular schedule of popular music groups from Bob Dylan to the Rolling Stones play here, plus large touring Broadway theater productions such as *Annie*, *Cats*, and *Les Misérables* offer regular performances, and there is an annual summer film festival.
➕ F4 ✉ 660 Peachtree Street ☎ 404/881-2100 🚇 North Avenue (N3) 🚌 2, 10, 45

GEORGIA DOME

The Atlanta Falcons (► 83) host other NFL teams in this mammoth enclosed stadium (seats 70,500 people) eight Sundays each year. During the rest of the year it is used for a variety of events ranging from motorcycle racing, concerts, conventions, and, recently, a Billy Graham crusade.
➕ E6 ✉ 1 Georgia Dome Drive ☎ 404/223-9200 🚇 Omni/Dome/GWCC (W1) 🚌 1, 11, 13, 18, 26, 50, 86

OMNI COLISEUM

Seating over 16,000 people, this is the home of Atlanta's professional basketball and hockey. When the teams aren't in attendance, it is used for large rock concerts, conventions, ice skating shows, and the circus.
➕ E6 ✉ 100 Techwood Drive behind CNN Center ☎ 404/681-2100 🚇 Omni/Dome/ GWCC (W1) 🚌 1, 11, 13, 18, 26, 50, 86

THEATERS

ACADEMY THEATRE

Atlanta's oldest theater company (since 1956) and the second oldest resident company in the United States performs original works by local and contemporary playwrights about modern themes and social problems.

✚ E5 ✉ 501 Means Avenue ☎ 404/525-4111 🚇 No subway/train station nearby 🚌 1, 26, 50

ACTOR'S EXPRESS

This critically acclaimed theater company housed in a renovated factory warehouse presents cutting-edge and eclectic productions by local and nationally renowned playwrights about modern themes and issues.

✚ E5 ✉ 887 West Marietta Street in King Plow Arts Center ☎ 404/607-7469 🚇 No subway/train station nearby 🚌 1, 11, 26, 50

ALLIANCE THEATRE

Considered one of the South's best professional theater companies, the Alliance performs everything from Shakespeare and Dickens' *A Christmas Carol* to the latest Broadway shows.

✚ F3 ✉ 1280 Peachtree Street (Woodruff Arts Center) ☎ 404/733-5000 🚇 Arts Center (N5) 🚌 10, 23, 35, 36, 48, 98

14TH STREET PLAYHOUSE

This Midtown theater is shared as a performance hall by several theater companies, including the Theatrical Outfit (☎ 404/872-0665) who produce original works with contemporary themes; Jomandi Productions (☎ 404/876-6346), the city's best African-American company specializing in works by contemporary black playwrights; Barking Dog Theater (☎ 404/885-1621) with innovative works by 20th-century playwrights; and Theatre Gael (☎ 404/876-1138) who produce plays by Celtic and Celtic-American writers.

✚ G3 ✉ 173 14th Street ☎ 404/873-1099 🚇 Midtown (N4), Arts Center (N5) 🚌 10, 31, 36

ONSTAGE ATLANTA & ABRACADABRA! CHILDREN'S THEATRE

This long established theater group offers a consistently interesting season of drama, comedies and musicals from its small and intimate theater. From the same location, the ABRACADABRA! Children's Theatre performs original plays and stage adaptations of works such as *Charlotte's Web* and *Winnie the Pooh*.

✚ G5 ✉ 420 Courtland Street ☎ 404/897-1802 🚇 Peachtree Center (N1), Civic Center (N2) 🚌 16, 46

7 STAGES THEATER

Utilizing contemporary playwrights, theater here is usually thought-provoking or controversial, covering a variety of social topics and taboos from racism, to the homeless, to homosexuality.

✚ J6 ✉ 1105 Euclid Avenue ☎ 404/522-0911 🚇 Inman Park-Reynoldstown (E3) 🚌 3, 48

Homegrown talent

Not world-renowned for its theater companies, Atlanta is more of a proving ground for actors, actresses, and playwrights who go on to bigger things in other cities. Many, who are in love with the city, prefer not to leave despite their great talent. You may not recognize their names on the marquee, but you are guaranteed of receiving good and innovative theater.

CLASSICAL MUSIC & DANCE

Music from the colleges

Outside the professional realm, one of the best places to hear classical music at very affordable prices is from the various orchestras and choral groups connected to the 30-odd colleges and universities in the area. The Emory University brass, chamber, and wind ensembles are quite good (☎ 404/727-6187), plus look for concerts by the University Symphony (☎ 404/651-3676) composed of members from several Atlanta colleges.

MUSIC

ATLANTA BOYS' CHOIR

This choir of 175 boys aged 5–14, modeled on the Vienna Boys' Choir, has been delighting international audiences since its beginning in 1956. The Grammy Award-winning group performs frequently in Atlanta and goes on an annual tour in Mexico and Europe. Its concerts in local churches are highlights of the Christmas season.

✉ Various venues
☎ 404/378-0064

ATLANTA OPERA ASSOCIATION

Local singers and musicians, augmented by international artists, perform 3–5 times per year, everything from the classics *Carmen* and *Lucia di Lammermoor* to more modern themes. It looks and sounds very professional, often getting good reviews from the local media. To help the audience, a screen placed above the stage displays a translation of the text from the original language.

⊞ F3 ✉ Usually at Symphony Hall (see below) ☎ 404/355-3311 ⓐ Arts Center (N5)
🚌 10, 23, 35, 36, 48, 98

ATLANTA SYMPHONY ORCHESTRA

This world-class and award-winning symphony orchestra, under the musical direction of Yoel Levi, recently celebrated its 50th anniversary. It performs its autumn–spring Master Season subscription series in the 1,800-seat Symphony Hall and has a Summer Pops Concert series outdoors at the Chastain Park Amphitheater (➤ 78), occasionally accompanying big-name artists who perform there. It also performs at other city locations for special events.

⊞ F3 ✉ 1280 Peachtree Street (Woodruff Arts Center)
☎ 404/733-5000 ⓐ Arts Center (N5) 🚌 10, 23, 35, 36, 48, 98

DANCE

THE ATLANTA BALLET COMPANY

The nation's oldest continually operating professional ballet company, founded in 1929, consistently receives international recognition for its high-quality productions of classical and contemporary works. Its annual rendition of Tchaikovsky's *The Nutcracker* is outstanding. Ticket prices, although generally expensive, are discounted greatly one hour before curtain time.

⊞ G5 ✉ Usually at the Atlanta Civic Center (➤ 78)
☎ 404/892-3303 ⓐ Civic Center (N2) 🚌 16, 46

INTERNATIONAL BALLET ROTARU

Romanian Pavel Rotaru, who spent a year with the Atlanta Ballet, leads this troupe with a series of classical and colorful ballet performances. They are a good alternative if the Atlanta Ballet is not in town.

⊞ F4 ✉ Usually at the Fox Theatre (➤ 41)
☎ 770/395-5322 ⓐ North Avenue (N3) 🚌 2, 10, 45

MUSIC CLUBS

Please note: the hours given for the clubs listed below are starting times for musical entertainment up to closing time. Those clubs that serve food and drink open earlier, so call in advance for their hours if you want to dine there. Establishments with live entertainment usually have a cover charge and/or drink minimum.

BLIND WILLIE'S
This is the best blues parlor in town for both music and atmosphere. Small, smoky, and always crowded, it features vocalists and bands playing Mississippi Delta and New Orleans-style blues, both vocal and instrumental pieces. Local musicians to rising stars and legendary greats can be found here. Unless you want to listen from outside, try to get here early.
➕ J4 ✉ 828 North Highland Avenue ☎ 404/873-2583 🕐 8P.M.–2A.M. daily 🚇 No subway/train station nearby 🚌 16

CHAMELEON CLUB
This Buckhead club is a frequent haunt of the under-30s crowd who come to hear new alternative and progressive rock bands, plus the blues featured on Wednesday nights. Dress is very casual, and there's a dance floor.
➕ Off grid F1 ✉ 3170 Peachtree Road ☎ 404/261-8004 🕐 Daily 11P.M.–4A.M. 🚇 No subway/train station nearby 🚌 23

DANTE'S DOWN THE HATCH
This jazz music club has been a favorite of locals and tourists alike for more than 20 years. You enter it through a streetside hatchway reminiscent of an old pirate ship, descending to lower decks where the nautical theme is continued with a ship's steering wheel, wharf front where the musicians play, and a moat with three live crocodiles.
➕ F7 ✉ Kenny's Alley in Underground Atlanta (➤ 29) ☎ 404/577-1800 🕐 Mon–Thu 5P.M.–midnight; Fri–Sat until 1A.M.; Sun until 11P.M. 🚇 Five Points (0) 🚌 3, 13, 17, 20, 42, 90, 97

EDDIE'S ATTIC
This upstairs club is the best place to hear local and national acoustic acts. Seating 225 people, it was one of the first gigs for the now famous Indigo Girls duo. The shows start early; it's an "all ages, no smoking" concert, and parents are allowed to bring their children to the club.
➕ Off grid K4 ✉ 515-B North McDonough Street in Decatur ☎ 404/377-4976 🕐 Daily 7P.M. and 9:30P.M. shows 🚇 Decatur (E6) 🚌 15, 17, 18, 96

THE POINT
This Little Five Points club is a showcase for up-and-coming rock, reggae, and progressive music groups in a small club setting.
➕ K5 ✉ 420 Moreland Avenue ☎ 404/659-3522 🕐 Daily 10P.M.–2A.M. 🚇 Inman Park–Reynoldstown (E3) 🚌 3, 48

Music, music, music
Atlanta has one of the best music club scenes in the nation with blues, country, folk, jazz, and every form of rock music heard in bars and clubs spread throughout the city and into the suburbs. Where it excels most is acoustic music and alternative-progressive rock fashioned after the famed REM, who began their career at the University of Georgia.

DANCE CLUBS

Hotlanta

Atlanta, nicknamed "Hotlanta" by the city's party animals, is the undisputed entertainment capital of the South, with a varied nightlife scene that has something for all ages, especially the 25–40 age group that makes up a large percentage of the population. Following their lead, begin with a meal at a chic restaurant, followed by a concert or music club show, and finish by dancing the early morning away.

AXYS

This upbeat, high-tech dance club in Midtown attracts a diverse crowd spanning more than one generation. Music is by disc jockeys with an occasional live band.

✚ G3 ✉ 1150-в Peachtree Street ☎ 404/607-0922 🕐 Fri 10P.M.–4A.M.; Sat until 3P.M. Ⓜ Midtown (N4), Arts Center (N5) 🚌 10, 37

BUCKBOARD COUNTRY MUSIC SHOWCASE

This is the largest country music dance club in metro Atlanta. Its house band pumps out the latest country rhythms and there's lots of good time dancing from the "Texas Two Step" and the latest country line dances. Occasional celebrities pop in for its Thursday night showcase of musicians.

✚ Off grid C1 ✉ 2080 Cobb Parkway in Windy Hill Plaza Shopping Center ☎ 770/955-7340 🕐 Mon–Fri 9P.M.–2A.M.; Sat until 3A.M. Ⓜ No subway/train station nearby 🚌 No bus service to here

CLUB ANYTIME

When the other clubs close, Atlantans come here for rock-around-the-clock dancing with popular music spun by a DJ.

✚ G3 ✉ 1055 Peachtree Street ☎ 404/607-8050 🕐 24-hours daily Ⓜ Midtown (N4) 🚌 10

JOHNNY'S HIDEAWAY

This is one of the most popular dance clubs in Atlanta for the over 40 set. Open every evening, it features ballroom dancing to big-band sounds of the 1940-50s, Presley ballads and golden oldies rock.

✚ Off grid F1 ✉ 3771 Roswell Road ☎ 404/233-8026 🕐 Sun–Fri 8P.M.–3A.M.; Sat until 4A.M. Ⓜ No subway/train station nearby 🚌 5

RUPERT'S

This dressy dance club attracts the Buckhead after-work crowd with its 12-piece orchestra playing big band, Top 40 hits and contemporary dance music. DJ hosted music is played between sets.

✚ Off grid H1 ✉ 3330 Piedmont Road ☎ 404/266-9834 🕐 Tue, Thu 5:30P.M.–2A.M.; Fri until 3A.M.; Sat 8P.M.–3A.M. Ⓜ Buckhead (N7) 🚌 5, 23

SOHO

SoHo is a take-off of New York City's nightclub scene, where your looks and the clothes you are wearing are more important than your money. So, dress to impress, or you probably won't get in. Once inside, expect high energy alternative and industrial music.

✚ F6 ✉ 187 Walton Street ☎ 404/222-0011 🕐 Fri–Sun 10P.M.–4A.M. Ⓜ Five points (0) 🚌 13

VELVET

This trendy Downtown club has developed a following among all age groups. Expect a different kind of music every night, and come to see celebrities like the band U2 who were spotted there recently.

✚ F7 ✉ 89 Park Place ☎ 404/681-9936 🕐 Mon 10P.M.–2A.M.; Wed, Fri, Sun until 4AM; Thu, Sat until 3AM Ⓜ Five Points (0) 🚌 17

SPECTATOR SPORTS

ATLANTA BRAVES

The Braves were the National League pennant-winners in 1991 and 1992. They currently play their home games at Atlanta-Fulton County Stadium where Hall of Fame star, Hank Aaron, broke Babe Ruth's record of 714 home runs (April 8, 1974). In 1997, the Braves will occupy the Olympic Stadium (85,000 capacity). After the 1996 Centennial Olympic Games, it will be converted to a baseball stadium seating 45,000–48,000 people.

➕ F8 ✉ 521 Capitol Avenue
☎ 404/249-6400 (Ticketmaster), 404/522-7630
🕐 Main season mid-Apr–Oct
Ⓢ Georgia State (E1)
🚌 Shuttle bus from Five Points station (0) for baseball games, or 17, 55, 90, 97, 100

ATLANTA FALCONS

The Falcons give Atlantans a chance to see professional football. They play in the National Football League's (NFL) national conference western division. Overall, the team has been a disappointment, usually playing 500 ball and not making the playoffs. The best part is seeing a game in the Georgia Dome with 70,000 plus other fans.

➕ E6 ✉ Georgia Dome (▶ 78) ☎ 404/223-8000
🕐 Main season Sep–Jan
Ⓢ Omni/Dome/GWCC (W1)
🚌 13, 51, 63

ATLANTA HAWKS

The Hawks play in the central division of the National Basketball Association's (NBA) eastern conference. Since this professional basketball team plays in the same division with the superior Chicago Bulls, it is rare for them to win a division championship, though they usually end up in the conference playoffs.

➕ E6 ✉ Omni Coliseum (▶ 78) ☎ 404/249-6400 (Ticketmaster), 404/827-DUNK
🕐 Main season Oct–Apr
Ⓢ Omni/Dome/GWCC (W1)
🚌 1, 11, 13, 18, 26, 50, 86

ATLANTA KNIGHTS

The International Hockey League (IHL) Knights won their league championship in 1994. As the top developmental league to provide new players and reserves for the professional National Hockey League's Tampa Bay Lightning team, this team's player roster is always in flux, which affects its performance and final finish.

➕ E6 ✉ Omni Coliseum (▶ 78) ☎ 404/525-8900
🕐 Main season Oct–May
Ⓢ Omni/Dome/GWCC (W1)
🚌 1, 11, 13, 18, 26, 50, 86

GEORGIA TECH YELLOW JACKETS

Participating in the tough Atlantic Coast Conference (ACC) of the NCAA, Georgia Tech teams give you high quality collegiate football (1990 national champion), basket-ball, baseball, tennis, wrestling, and other sports.

➕ F4, F5 ✉ Georgia Institute of Technology campus (between North Avenue and 10th Street)
☎ 404/894-5447
Ⓢ North Avenue (N3)
🚌 13

Annual sporting events

Atlanta is host to several annual sporting events including the Peachtree Road Race run on July 4 (14 km), the Coca-Cola 500, a professional stock-car race (March) at the Atlanta International Raceway (☎ 404/946-4211); the Bell South Atlanta Classic, a four-day tournament (May) with the world's best golfers (☎ 404/951-8777); and the AT&T Challenge, a tennis tournament (April) featuring the world's top-ranked men players (☎ 404/881-8811), including past winners Boris Becker and Ivan Lendl.

LUXURY HOTELS

Modern luxury

The majority of Atlanta's most expensive establishments are found primarily Downtown and in Buckhead, with a few in the Midtown area and along the north perimeter of the city. Architecturally, all of them are modern, the oldest being the Hyatt Regency Atlanta that opened in 1967, the remainder being built primarily in the 1980s. All are owned by international hotel chains. You can expect to pay $160 or more for a double or twin-bedded room.

ATLANTA MARRIOTT MARQUIS

Downtown's newest luxury hotel is the largest capacity hotel (► 50) in Atlanta with 1,671 rooms. The hotel has an efficient staff and numerous amenities, including five restaurants and a full service health club.

➕ F6 ✉ 265 Peachtree Center Avenue ☎ 404/521-0000 or 800/328-9290; fax 404/586-6299 🚇 Peachtree Center (N1) 🚌 16, 31, 46

HOTEL NIKKO ATLANTA

A double level lobby facing a courtyard with a Japanese garden and cascading 35 foot waterfall invites you into this hotel. Its two restaurants with Mediterranean French and Japanese cuisine are among the city's best.

➕ Off grid H1 ✉ 3300 Peachtree Road at Piedmont Road ☎ 404/365-8100 or 800/645-5687; fax 404/233-5686 🚇 Buckhead (N7), Lenox (NE7) 🚌 5, 23

OCCIDENTAL GRAND HOTEL

This elegant hotel offers affordable luxury with its lavish marble-tiled atrium lobby, two outstanding restaurants and spacious rooms.

➕ F3 ✉ 75 14th Street ☎ 404/881-9898 or 800/952-0702; fax 404/873-4692 🚇 Arts Center (N5) 🚌 98

OMNI HOTEL AT CNN CENTER

This hotel is in a prime location if you are attending events at the World Congress Center, Omni Coliseum or Georgia Dome. A MARTA station next to the Coliseum puts other Atlanta sights just a few minutes away.

➕ F6 ✉ 100 CNN Center ☎ 404/659-0000 or 800/843-6664; fax 404/525-5050 🚇 Omni/Dome/WCC (W1) 🚌 1, 11, 13, 18, 26, 50, 86

RITZ-CARLTON ATLANTA

The Ritz reminds you of the best luxury hotels with its coolly efficient service. Rooms are spacious and pleasantly furnished with reproduction antiques.

➕ F6 ✉ 181 Peachtree Street ☎ 404/659-0400 or 800/241-3333; fax 404/688-0400 🚇 Peachtree Center (N1) 🚌 10, 31

RITZ-CARLTON BUCKHEAD

Decorated with antiques, this elegant hotel offers excellent service, style and location. Lenox Square Mall and Phipps Plaza are both opposite the hotel. Its Dining Room is Atlanta's only 5-star restaurant (► 66).

➕ Off grid K1 ✉ 3434 Peachtree Road ☎ 404/237-2700 or 800/241-3333; fax 404/239-0078 🚇 Buckhead (N7), Lenox (NE7) 🚌 23, 25, 47, 48, 85, 92, 140

WESTIN PEACHTREE PLAZA HOTEL

This 73-story, cylindrical glass tower is the second tallest hotel in North America. Rooms above the 40th story offer great views of Downtown.

➕ F6 ✉ 210 Peachtree Street ☎ 404/659-1400 or 800/228-3000; fax 404/589-7424 🚇 Peachtree Center (N1) 🚌 10, 13, 31

MID-RANGE HOTELS

ANSLEY INN

This handsome 3-story brick Tudor mansion, now used as a bed and breakfast inn, features oversize guest rooms with private baths, furnished with Chinese porcelains and antiques.

➕ G3 ✉ 253 15th Street ☎ 404/872-9000 or 800/446-5416; fax 404/892-2318 🚇 Arts Center (N5) 🚌 10, 31, 36

DAYS INN HOTEL– PEACHTREE

Located opposite the Fox Theatre, this hotel is a bargain, if for location alone. Housed in a former 12-story, 1924 luxury apartment building, its sumptuous lobby features an 18th-century Georgian brass chandelier suspended from a lofty mahogany panelled ceiling, with reproduction antiques in the rooms.

➕ F4 ✉ 683 Peachtree Street ☎ 404/874-9200 or 800/325-2525; fax 404/873-4245 🚇 North Avenue (N3) 🚌 2, 10, 45

DOUBLETREE HOTEL ATLANTA

This ultramodern hotel on the north perimeter of Atlanta gives a taste of luxury for an affordable price (high end of moderate range). Its spacious rooms, efficient service, first-class restaurant, plus privileges for all its guests at a nearby full service fitness club, make it a popular choice.

➕ Off grid G1 ✉ Seven Concourse Parkway ☎ 404/395-3900 or 800/222-TREE; fax 404/395-3935 🚇 Dunwoody (N9) 🚌 150

MARRIOTT RESIDENCE INN MIDTOWN

This suites-only hotel resembles a classy apartment building. Each suite has a fully equipped kitchen, comfortable reproduction antique furniture, full-length mirrors, marble tiled bathrooms, ceiling fans, and televisions in every room. A continental breakfast is served in a room off the lobby.

➕ F3 ✉ 1041 West Peachtree Street ☎ 404/872-8885 or 800/331-3131; fax 404/872-8888 🚇 Midtown (N4) 🚌 37

QUALITY INN HABERSHAM

The attractive rooms in this small Downtown hotel are furnished with extra chairs, sofa and walk-in wardrobe, a good bargain in an expensive area. A complimentary continental breakfast is served every morning.

➕ F6 ✉ 330 Peachtree Street ☎ 404/577-1980 or 800/241-4288; fax 404/688-3706 🚇 Peachtree Center (N1) 🚌 10, 31, 46

TERRACE GARDEN INN BUCKHEAD

This stylish hotel is in a prime location opposite Lenox Square Mall. Its comfortable rooms are furnished with reproduction French and English antique furniture, and it has a full service fitness area, swimming pool and tennis courts.

➕ Off grid K1 ✉ 3405 Lenox Road ☎ 404/261-9250 or 800/241-8260, fax 404/848-7301 🚇 Lenox (NE7) 🚌 23, 25, 47, 48, 85, 92, 140

Hotel choice

Finding a hotel in Atlanta shouldn't be a problem, but don't expect a room without an advance reservation if you want to stay in Downtown, Midtown, or Buckhead, since this is the prime turf of business people and those attending conventions. As an alternative, consider the north "Perimeter" (along I-285 between I-75 and I-85), which has several excellent hotels in all price categories and size. On average you can expect to pay $85–$159 for a double or twin-bedded room.

BUDGET ACCOMMODATIONS

Motel rooms

Inexpensive lodging in Atlanta is also available from several national motel chains, nondescript 1–4 story structures usually bordering the interstate highways. Double occupancy rooms with private baths, one large bed or two double beds, a television, desk, and other basic amenities are in the $50–$80 range. The best low-cost chains include Days Inn, Hampton Inn, La Quinta Inn, Red Roof Inn and Courtyard by Marriott.

BARCLAY HOTEL

This older hotel with tastefully decorated rooms is located a few blocks from Peachtree Street. Convenient for Downtown sights, its Celebrity Café is known for its waffles and fried chicken.

✚ F6 ✉ 89 Luckie Street ☎ 404/524-7991; fax 404/525-0672 🚇 Peachtree Center (N1) 🚌 13

BEST WESTERN AMERICAN HOTEL

Though on the high end of the inexpensive range, this older hotel, opposite the bus station and behind the gleaming Westin Peachtree Plaza Hotel, is a good choice if you are seeking location and value. Famous guests who have stayed here before more modern hotels were built include Elvis Presley and Richard Nixon.

✚ F6 ✉ 160 Spring Street ☎ 404/688-8600 ; fax 404/658-9458 🚇 Peachtree Center (N1) 🚌 13

CHESHIRE MOTOR INN

This family-run motor lodge, between Downtown and Buckhead, is a favorite for its inexpensive prices and personal touches, such as free coffee and newspapers every morning. The Colonnade Restaurant (▶ 62), one of the best for southern cuisine, is on the same premises.

✚ Off grid H1 ✉ 1865 Cheshire Bridge Road ☎ 404/872-9628 or 800/827-9628; fax 404/875-0640 🚇 No subway/train station nearby 🚌 27

EMORY INN

This older hotel tucked into a forest near Emory University provides a peaceful setting away from the hustle and bustle of the commercial business districts, yet if you have to get there, it is only a short drive away.

✚ Off grid K2 ✉ 1641 Clifton Road ☎ 404/712-6700 or 800/933-6679; fax 404/712-6701 🚇 No subway/train station nearby 🚌 6

HAMPTON INN BUCKHEAD

Although the rooms are not large or fancy, the location and price are right, plus there's an indoor pool and an all-you-can-eat continental breakfast held in the lobby every morning. This chain also guarantees your stay: if you're not 100 percent satisfied, they will refund your money.

✚ Off grid H1 ✉ 3398 Piedmont Road ☎ 404/233-5656 or 800/HAMPTON; fax 404/237-4688 🚇 Buckhead (N7) 🚌 5

LENOX INN

This attractive motel, opposite Lenox Square Mall, assures you of good service at a very affordable price. The rooms are basic, but clean and well furnished with modern amenities. The fitness room and exercise facilities of the next door Terrace Garden Inn are available to guests of this establishment.

✚ Off grid K1 ✉ 3387 Lenox Road ☎ 404/261-5500 or 800/578-7878; fax 404/261-6140 🚇 Lenox (NE7) 🚌 23, 25, 47, 48, 85, 92, 140

ATLANTA
travel facts

ARRIVING & DEPARTING

When to go

- Spring and autumn are the best seasons to visit Atlanta.
- April is "blossom time" for a wide range of shrubs, trees, and flowers.
- October temperatures are moderate and the city is once again filled with color as the tree leaves change from green to brilliant shades of red, orange, and yellow.
- Most outdoor arts and crafts fairs are held from mid-September to mid-November.

Climate

- Average summer temperatures range from 83 to 88°F (28–30°C), often with 80–90 per cent humidity.
- Winter temperatures rarely dip below 40°F (4°C) during the day, but with higher humidity, the dampness often makes it seem colder. Snow and ice are rare.
- Spring and autumn temperatures are 65–84°F (18–29°C) during the day.
- There are violent thunderstorms in the late spring and summer.
- Weather forecast, temperature and time: ☎ 404/455-7141.

Arriving by air

- The major gateway to Atlanta is Hartsfield Atlanta International Airport (☎ 404/530-6830), the second busiest airport in the United States in terms of daily passengers.
- Hartsfield has daily nonstop flights to 150 domestic destinations.
- An automated, high-speed, mini-subway train rushes passengers from the various arrival concourses to the main terminal building and baggage area. Moving sidewalks link the concourse subway waiting areas.

- Transportation into the city is provided by the MARTA Rapid Rail system (see Public Transportation), taxis, shuttle buses, and rental car companies.
- Major American carriers serving Atlanta include America West (☎ 800/235-9292), American (☎ 800/433-7300), Air South (☎ 800/247-7688), Continental (☎ 800/525-0280), Delta (☎ 800/221-1212), Northwest (☎ 800/225-2525), TWA (☎ 800/221-2000), United (☎ 800/241-6522), and USAir (☎ 800/428-4322).
- For inexpensive, no-frills flights, contact Kiwi International (☎ 800/538-5494), based in Newark and New York; MarkAir (☎ 800/627-5247), based in Anchorage, Alaska; Midwest Express (☎ 800/452-2022), based in Milwaukee, which serves 45 U.S. cities in the Midwest and on both coasts, including Atlanta; Private Jet (☎ 404/231-7571, 800/546-7571, or 800/949-9400), based in Atlanta; and Valu-Jet (☎ 404/994-8538 or 800/825-8538), also based in Atlanta.

Arriving by bus and train

- Greyhound Bus Lines (✉ 81 International Boulevard; ☎ 800/231-2222, 404/522-6300) links Atlanta with other major U.S. cities.
- Amtrak train service (✉ 1688 Peachtree Street; ☎ 800/872-7245) has regular services to and from Birmingham, Mobile, New Orleans, Greenville (South Carolina), Charlotte, Washington, D.C., Baltimore, Philadelphia, and New York.

Arriving by car

- Atlanta is easily accessible from several locations by the interstate highway system (see below) or

major highways that enter the city.
- Avoid these roads and highways during the rush hour (6:30–9A.M. and 3:30–7P.M.).

City layout
- Atlanta is circled by interstate highway I-285, known by locals as the "Perimeter", and crossed east–west by I-20 and north–south by I-75 and I-85.
- North of the MARTA Five Points station, Peachtree Street bisects the city, traveling up through Downtown, Midtown and Buckhead (now Peachtree Road) to the suburb of Chamblee, just inside the north "Perimeter."

ESSENTIAL FACTS

Travel insurance
- Make sure you have a policy covering accident, medical expenses, personal liability, trip cancellation, delayed departure and loss or theft of personal property.
- Before you leave, make sure you will be covered if you have a pre-existing medical condition or are pregnant; your insurers may not pay for routine or continuing treatment or may require a note from your doctor certifying your fitness to travel.
- Travel insurance covering baggage, health, and trip cancellation or interruptions is available from **Access America**, (Box 90315, Richmond, VA 23286, ☎ 804/285-3300 or 800/284-8300), **Carefree Travel Insurance** (Box 9366, 100 Garden City Plaza, Garden City, NY 11530, ☎ 516/294-0220 or 800/323-3149), **Near Services** (Box 1339, Calumer City, Il, 60409, ☎ 708/868-6700 or 800/654-6700),

Tele-Trip (Mutual of Omaha Plaza, Box 31716, Omaha, NE 68131, ☎ 800/228-9792), **Travel Insured International** (Box 280568, East Hartford, CT 06128-0568, ☎ 203/528-7663 or 800/243-3174), **Travel Guard International** (1145 Clark St., Stevens Point, WI 54481, ☎ 715/345-0505 or 800/826-1300), and **Wallach & Company** (107 W. Federal St., Box 480, Middleburg, VA 22117, ☎ 703/687-3166 or 800/237-6615).

Average opening hours
- Department stores and malls: Mon–Sat 9:30–9, Sun noon–5:30
- Specialty shops: Mon–Sat 9:30–6
- Supermarkets: daily 24-hours (some)
- Banks: Mon–Fri 9–5; Sat 9–noon, for a few locations
- Museums: Mon–Sat 10–5, Sun noon–5
- Offices: Mon–Fri 8:30–5
- Post offices: Mon–Fri 8:30–5; Sat 9–1 for a few locations.

Public holidays
- New Year's Day (January 1)
- Martin Luther King, Jr. Day (third Monday in January)
- President's Day (third Monday in February)
- Confederate Memorial Day (April 26)
- Memorial Day (last Monday in May)
- Independence Day (July 4)
- Labor Day (first Monday in September)
- Thanksgiving Day (fourth Thursday in November)
- Christmas Day (December 25).
- Banks, post offices, and most government agencies are closed for these holidays, although most museums and shops are open.

89

Money matters

- Nearly all banks have Automatic Teller Machines (ATMs), which accept cards registered in other countries that are linked to the Cirrus or Plus networks. Before leaving home, check which network your cards are linked to and ensure your personal identification number is valid. For specific Cirrus locations in the United States and Canada, call 800/424-7787. For U.S. Plus locations, call 800/843-7587 and enter the area code and first three digits of the number you are calling from (or of the calling area where you want an ATM).
- Credit cards are a widely accepted and a secure alternative to cash. Visa, MasterCard, American Express, Diner's Card, and Discover are the most commonly used cards.
- Traveler's checks function like cash in all but small shops; $20 and $50 denominations are the most useful. Don't bother trying to exchange these at the bank—it is more trouble than it's worth and commissions are high.
- Traveler's checks and foreign currency can be exchanged at Thomas Cook-Wachovia Bank of Georgia (🕐 Mon–Fri 9–7, Sat and Sun 4-7) foreign exchange counter located directly opposite the airport's international airline ticket counters. Wachovia, NationsBank, First Union and other local banks also have a foreign exchange counter at their Downtown offices and selected other branches.
- You can send or receive a MoneyGram from American Express (☎ 800/926-9400) for up to $20,000. MoneyGram agents are in more than 70 countries. Western Union (☎ 800/325-6000) is linked to 22,000 locations in 78 countries.

Etiquette

- Southerners are generally friendly and may greet you on the street even though you are a stranger. But beware of where this happens, as Downtown is notorious for pickpockets who will beg or try to engage you in conversation so they can lift your wallet.
- Don't flaunt valuables such as money, cameras, jewelry.
- Smoking is forbidden on public transportation and in most public buildings and shops. Restaurants usually have both a smoking and nonsmoking section.

Single travelers

- It is generally safe to travel alone during the day as long as you stick to the main streets and safe neighborhoods. (Note: housing projects and slums are adjacent to Downtown Atlanta on all sides except the north. Don't venture into them alone.) When in doubt, ask.
- At night anywhere, it is wise to travel in a group of three or more, or for women to travel with a male escort.
- Exercise special caution when Downtown at night and at nightclubs anywhere.

Places of worship

- Churches abound in Atlanta.
- The majority of believers are Christian divided between many Protestant denominations, the highest percentage being Baptist, followed by Presbyterian, Methodist, Church of God, Lutheran, Pentecostal, Episcopalian, and several other smaller sects. These churches meet for worship on Sunday mornings.

- There are also places of worship for Roman Catholics, Jews, and Muslims.

Student travelers

- With 36 universities and colleges, Atlanta provides numerous learning opportunities for students, plus admission discounts are available with a valid student ID card at various music clubs, museums, and tourist sights.
- The Atlanta Convention and Visitors Bureau (✉ 233 Peachtree Street, Suite 2000, Atlanta, GA 30303; ☎ 800/ATLANTA, 404/ 222- 6688) has an "International Youth Travel Program" where students are given discounted rates ($25–$45) at 11 hotels.
- The American Youth Hostel at 223 Ponce de Leon Avenue (☎ 404/872-8844) has inexpensive lodgings for students.

Travel agencies

- For names of reputable agencies in your area, contact the American Society of Travel Agents (1101 King St., Suite 200, Alexandria, VA 22314, ☎ 703/739-2782).

Rest rooms

- Rest Rooms are reasonably plentiful, lcoated at all tourist sights, shopping malls, deparment stores, libraries, fast food eateries, and restaurants. There is no charge for their use, but cleanliness does vary greatly.

Senior Citizens

- Contact the American Association of Retired Persons (AARP, 601E St. NW, Washington, DC 20049, ☎ 202/434-2277; $8 per person or couple annually) for information about member discounts and

road-service aid. For other discounts on lodgings, car rentals, and other travel products, along with magazines and newsletters, contact the National Council of Senior Citizens (1331 F St. NW, Washington, DC 20004, ☎ 202/347-8800; membership $12 annually) and Mature Outlook magazine (6001 N. Clark St., Chicago, IL 60660, ☎ 312/465-6466 or 800/336-6330; subscription $9.95 annually).

Public Transportation

- To use public transportation, look for the word MARTA (Metropolitan Atlanta Rapid Transit Association) at bus stops and trainstations.
- You will find letters and numbers in brackets after the names of MARTA stops. These indicate both the direction of the line and the number of stops away from Five Points (0), the hub of the network.

MARTA Rapid Rail

- Clean, efficient and safe "Rapid Rail" trains run beneath Downtown and Midtown Atlanta as a subway (underground) and primarily on elevated tracks throughout the rest of the city.
- The east–west line stops at 14 stations from Hightower near the west side of I-285 to Indian Creek just beyond the east side of I-285; the short Proctor Creek extension line branches beyond the Ashby station (🚇 W3) to one additional stop.
- The north–south line, with 17 stations, runs from Hartsfield Atlanta International Airport to Doraville, a suburb just north-west of the I-85 and I-285 intersection.

- Both main lines cross at the Downtown Five Points station where a transfer can be made free to the other line. Station entrances, exits, platforms, and directions are clearly marked.
- The cost to ride a MARTA train or bus is $1.50. Station turnstiles require exact change (excluding pennies or half dollars) or tokens can be purchased from machines at the station entrance.
- For transferring to a bus line at the departure stop, push the white "Transfer" button after inserting your money in the turnstile. There is a designated slot on the turnstile to insert discount cards (make sure you retrieve it).
- Trains run 4:35 A.M.–1:17 A.M. with 8–15 minute intervals between trains depending on the line, day and time; drivers announce each stop.
- From the airport (space is provided for luggage) to Five Points takes 15 minutes, 17 minutes to Peachtree Center and 30 minutes to Lenox Square Mall.
- Free parking is available at most suburban stations.
- MARTA has a good security record, with its own police force. Every station is monitored by a closed circuit television system.

MARTA buses

- MARTA operates a fleet of 700 buses on 150 routes covering 1,500 miles.
- Outside of I-285, service is limited.
- Selected buses stop at most rapid rail stations and at hundreds of street locations.
- To identify a street bus-stop, look for an approximately four-foot high, slender, white cement post with BUS STOP carved into it; some stops also have a small covered area or bench.

- A special machine accepts $1 bills and there is a slot for coins.
- Discount pass cards must be shown to the driver upon entering the bus and a transfer slip, if needed, must be requested from the driver

Schedule & map information

- Schedule and route maps are available for all the MARTA rail lines and buses at the Five Points station and in limited stock at the other stations.
- Any other questions can be answered at the information booths manned by MARTA employees or write to them at 2424 Piedmont Road, Atlanta, GA 30324 (☎ 404/848-4711).

Ticket discounts

- A two- or three-day weekend pass ($6 and $8) gives unlimited travel on both trains and buses.
- Weekly TransCards, good for seven days of unlimited travel, cost only $12; monthly TransCards are $45.
- Passes and cards can be purchased at the *Ride Store* at the Five Points station and at the business office of several area grocery stores and businesses.

Taxis

- Unlike other cities where a cab can be hailed off the street, you have to call for a taxi in Atlanta, or go to a hotel or MARTA station where they congregate.
- Taxi fares start at $1.50 for the first one-sixth mile and 20¢ for each additional one-sixth mile. Each additional person is charged a $1.
- For any destination within the Downtown Convention Zone (bounded by Boulevard, 14th Street, Northside Drive and Atlanta-Fulton County Stadium),

a flat fare of $4 for one person or $2 per person for two or more passengers is charged.

- Between the airport and Downtown hotels, it is a fixed rate of $15 for one person, $8 each for two people, $6 each for three people.
- 24-hour service: Checker Cab (☎ 404/351-1111); Buckhead Safety Cab (☎ 404/233-1152).

MEDIA & COMMUNICATION

Telephones

- At press time, Atlanta was preparing for a new area code, 770, to be used for most numbers outside the I-285 Perimeter. Numbers inside the Perimeter generally will retain the 404 code. This guide reflects the anticipated division.
- The long-distance services of AT&T, MCI, and Sprint make calling home relatively convenient and let you avoid hotel surcharges; typically, you dial an 800 number in the United States.
- Information: ☎ 411.

Post offices

- There are more than 100 post offices in the Atlanta area.

Newspapers & magazines

- The *Atlanta Journal* is the city's daily morning newspaper and the *Atlanta Constitution* is the evening edition.
- *USA Today, Wall Street Journal,* and *New York Times* are available at some newsstands and bookstores.
- *Creative Loafing,* a weekly paper, has good information about entertainment. It is distributed for free at MARTA stations, restaurants, and stores. Free monthlies include *Where Atlanta,*

Atlanta Now and *Key Atlanta,* distributed by hotels and the tourism bureau.

- The monthly *Atlanta Magazine* is the official city magazine with stories about local personalities, restaurants, fashion, forth-coming events.

Radio stations

- There are numerous commercial radio stations to choose from on both AM and FM dials, covering a gamut of musical tastes and talk show subjects. The following offer a good selection
- AM: WPLO 610: Country; WGST 640: News/Talk; WCNN 680: Sports/Talk; W5B 750: News/Talk; WQXI 790: Music/Talk; WNIV 970: Christian Talk/Music; WGKA 1190: Classical FM: WABE 90.1: National Public Radio/Classical; WCLK 91.9: Jazz/Soul; WZGC 92.9: Classical Rock; WPCH 94.9: Light Rock; WPCH 94.9: Light Rock; WKL5 96.1: Album Rock; WFOX 97.1: Oldies; WKHX 101.5: Country; WVEE 103.3: Top: 40/Soul.

Television

- Atlanta has a good selection of 24-hour television viewing, including the major networks— ABC, CBS, and NBC—plus the Fox Network, PBS, and several independent stations.
- Most hotels have cable television, which offers a very wide range of selections including TBS, CNN (based in Atlanta), HBO (movies), Disney Channel, and ESPN (sports).

EMERGENCIES

Sensible precautions

- Atlanta has a high crime rate,

though a large percentage is drug- or domestic-related.

- Tourist sights are safe during the day, but extra caution needs to be taken at night, especially in Downtown and Midtown.
- Stick to main streets, avoid parks, alleys and other isolated areas, don't wear visible jewelry and don't carry large sums of cash.
- On subway trains, sit in the first car, nearest to the driver.

Lost property

- If you've lost a valuable item, contact the Atlanta Police Department at 658-6600. You will need its report for an insurance claim.
- For a lost credit card, contact the issuing company immediately.

Medical treatment

- Emergency: ☎ 911 for an ambulance.
- Hospital 24-hour emergency rooms (when an ambulance is not needed):
  Downtown: Grady Memorial Hospital (✉ 80 Butler Street; ☎ 404/616-4307)
  Midtown: Crawford Long Hospital (✉ 550 Peachtree Street N.E.; ☎ 404/ 686-4411,emergencies ☎ 404/892- 4411); Georgia Baptist Medical Center (✉ 300 Boulevard N.E.; ☎ 404/653-4000, emergencies ☎ 404/653-4136).
  Buckhead: Piedmont Hospital (✉ 1968 Peachtree Road N.W.;

Doctors and dentists

- The Medical Association of Atlanta (☎ 404/881-1714 ⓞ Mon–Thu 9–4, Fri 9–3) has a referral service for over 2,000 Atlanta physicians in every field of expertise.
- The Georgia Dental Association of Atlanta (☎ 404/458-6166; ⓞ Mon– Fri 8:30–5) will refer

you to a dentist closest to your hotel for any special needs.

Medicines

- 24-hour pharmacy: Big B Drug (✉ 1061 Ponce de Leon Avenue, ☎ 404/876-0381).
- Kroger supermarkets, a 24-hour grocery chain with over 50 Atlanta locations, have a full-service pharmacy open daily (except Christmas) 9–9.

Emergency telephone numbers

- Ambulance, fire, and police: ☎ 911
- Poison control center: ☎ 616-9000
- Rape crisis center: ☎ 616-4861

VISITOR INFORMATION

- Contact the **Atlanta Convention & Visitors Bureau** (ACVB, 233 Peachtree St., Suite 2000, 30303, ☎ 404/521-6600, 404/222-6688 [automated information service], or 800/ATLANTA) for a city map and brochures about all major sights and upcoming events. Ask for their EXPLOR-A-CARD, which can be used for discounts at selected sights, hotels, restaurants, and shops.
- The **Georgia Department of Industry, Trade and Tourism**, (Box 1776, 30301, ☎ 404/656-3590 or 800/847-4842, Fax 404/656-3567) can answer most of your questions about travel in the state.
- The free, 176-page *Georgia on My Mind* magazine offers a wealth of information.
- The **Welcome South Visitors Center** (200 Spring St., ☎ 404/224-2000) has information and exhibits about Atlanta, the region, and the Olympics, besides a Thomas Cook office, AAA Club South, and other services.

INDEX

ACKNOWLEDGMENTS

The Automobile Association would like to thank the following photographers,
libraries and associations for their assistance in the preparation of this book.
THE ATLANTA CYCLORAMA (T WARREN) 12, 25a ATLANTA
LANDMARKS 1994 (KEVIN C ROSE) 7 CENTER FOR PUPPETRY ARTS
5a, 45 REX FEATURES LTD 9 THE SCIENCE & TECHNOLOGY
MUSEUM OF ATLANTA 39a SOUTHEASTERN RAILWAY MUSEUM 54
All remaining pictures are held in the Association's own library (AA PHOTO
LIBRARY) and were taken by ETHEL DAVIES

Copy-editor: *Lynn Bresler*   Verifier: *Giselle Rothwell*
Indexer: *Marie Lorimer*   Original design: *Design FX*